TURN IMPOSTOR SYNDROME
INTO YOUR
Superpower

TURN IMPOSTOR SYNDROME INTO YOUR *Superpower*

HOW TO REWIRE YOUR BRAIN

TO STOP PLAYING SMALL AND

Unapologetically GO AFTER

WHAT YOU WANT

CHRISTINE CORCORAN

Copyright © 2025 Christine Corcoran

No part of this publication may be reproduced, stored in a retrieval system, or transmitted in any form or by any means—electronic, photocopying, recording, or otherwise—without prior written permission, except in the case of brief excerpts in critical reviews and articles.

For permission requests, contact the author at christine@christinecorcorancom.au

All rights reserved.

Cover Designer: Brodi-Rose Newsome
https://www.brodi-rose.com/

ISBN: 978-1-7638123-0-7

Publisher: Self Published
Christine Corcoran
Ingram Spark

The author disclaims responsibility for adverse effects or consequences from the misapplication or injudicious use of the information contained in this book. Mention of resources and associations does not imply an endorsement.

Disclaimer:
The material in this publication is in the nature of general comment only and neither purports nor intends to be advice. Readers should not act on the basis of any matter in this publication without considering (and if appropriate taking) professional advice with due regard to their own particular circumstances. The author and publisher expressly disclaim all and any liability to any person, whether a purchaser of this publication or not, in respect of anything and the consequences of anything done or omitted to be done by any such person in reliance, whether whole or partial upon the whole or any part of the contents of this publication.

THIS BOOK IS DEDICATED TO THE ACTION TAKERS, THE AMBITIOUS WOMEN IN BUSINESS WHO STRIVE FOR GREATNESS EVERY DAY. THE ONES WHO CARE ABOUT LEAVING A POSITIVE IMPACT ON THOSE THEY ENCOUNTER AND WHO CHOOSE TO LIVE A LIFE OF EXPANSION.

Contents

PREFACE   3

INTRODUCTION

1. WE ALL EXPERIENCE THE IMPOSTOR SYNDROME   21
2. WHAT IS IMPOSTOR SYNDROME, REALLY?   47
3. CAUSES OF IMPOSTOR SYNDROME   55
4. OTHER SYMPTOMS OF IMPOSTOR SYNDROME   75

STEP ONE: EXPECT IT

5. ARIZONA   85
6. OUR RELATIONSHIP WITH FEAR   93
7. THE THREE FEAR RESPONSES   103
8. TRANSMUTE THE FEAR   107
9. UPDATE YOUR IDENTITY   117

STEP TWO: EMBRACE IT

10. LEARNING NOT TO RUN FROM REJECTION   131
11. FLIP THE SCRIPT   137

12	BUILD A BANK OF EVIDENCE	163
13	DO HARD THINGS	177
14	GET LEVERAGE ON YOURSELF	185
15	CELEBRATING YOUR WINS	205
16	LEARNING TO ACKNOWLEDGE YOURSELF	215
17	ACT FROM YOUR FUTURE SELF	225

STEP THREE: SEEK IT OUT

18	LAGUNA BEACH	233
19	CHOOSING CROWTH	237
20	EVEN HIGH ACHIEVERS PLAY SMALL	251
21	EXPANSION GOALS	255
22	THE IMPOSTOR SYNDROME IS YOUR SUPERPOWER	273

| ACKNOWLEDGMENTS | 283 |
| ABOUT THE AUTHOR | 285 |

Turn Impostor Syndrome into Your Superpower is a transformational guide that redefines how to approach persistent feelings of self-doubt, avoidance, and inadequacy while striving for more in life. Rather than focusing on overcoming Imposter Syndrome, this book empowers readers to harness it as a powerful growth tool. By shifting their perspective, readers learn how to use the Impostor Syndrome to push beyond their comfort zone, tackle challenges head-on, and pursue goals with renewed confidence.

Unlike most books that view the Impostor Syndrome as a hurdle, this book shows readers how it can become the catalyst for unlocking true potential. Through relatable stories, real-life experiences, and neuroscience backed strategies, renowned Business Mindset Coach Christine Corcoran leads readers on a roadmap showing them how to not only embrace the Imposter Syndrome they experience, but turn it into their own superpower.

CHRISTINE CORCORAN

Through engaging activations, mindset shifts and personalised stories, Corcoran demonstrates how readers can get out of their own way and unapologetically go after what they want.

ON THE OTHER SIDE OF
IMPOSTER SYNDROME, YOUR MOST
EXTRAORDINARY LIFE AWAITS.

Preface

The idea for this book came while I was writing another book. Crazy I know, but like any true entrepreneur, we're never short on ideas. The important thing is knowing which ones to take action on. I finished another book of over 100,000 words and in the process of looking for a publisher, I had a conversation that changed my trajectory: speaking with a potential publisher I determined that my first book needed to be a different concept, another idea I had been sitting on. For years, I have taught my framework on overcoming the Impostor Syndrome by learning to turn it into your superpower. To my clients, to online groups and communities, on stages, and more I would speak about the doors that open when you stop shutting them on yourself. I realised that everyone could relate to the feelings of Imposter Syndrome. In my mind I had a simple framework that could be so powerful and useful. I decided after the conversation that my first book needed to be an explanation of this framework and its benefits for business and life. So, I got to work getting it out of my head and onto paper.

My intention for this book and for you, is to transform the way you experience the Impostor Syndrome and help you ignite unstoppable belief in yourself so you can unapologetically go after your dreams. After coaching hundreds of people in the past 7 + years in business, this has always been my intention.

I want you to believe in your potential so unabashedly that you blow your own mind with what you create in life. Too many of us doubt ourselves and let the inner chatter of our minds keep us playing small and it cripples our potential, myself included. Even as a business and mindset coach, I too struggle with the Impostor Syndrome, and other mind traps that keep us in our comfort zone where it's safe. Nothing great is ever achieved in our comfort zone, we all know that, which means we all need to become great at spotting the self sabotaging thoughts of Imposter Syndrome and fill our tool boxes with new strategies to overcome them. It's always those who are brave enough to face their fears head on and move through them that

PREFACE

create extraordinary lives — and they are not any different to you and me — they just put these tools into action.

Together I hope to fill your toolbox with new practical strategies that are neuroscience-backed coaching tools I teach my clients every day so you too can create an extraordinary life.

A few important things before we get started.

THE USE OF "THE" IN FRONT OF IMPOSTOR SYNDROME

As a coach, I keep an eye out for identity beliefs. An identity belief is a belief/truth that we apply to our identity (to who we are as people) and these beliefs can be particularly difficult to overcome, so over the years when supporting hundreds of women in my coaching business, when a client of mine came up against Impostor Syndrome it was helpful for them to see the Impostor Syndrome as something separate to who they are as a person. Impostor Syndrome is something we experience, but it's not who we are or something we are defined by. The fear-based thoughts although convincing, are often not even true. Yet because we feel it and think it, we can often take Imposter Syndrome on board as who we are as a person, making it part of our identity. So throughout the text you'll see me use *the* in front of Impostor Syndrome even though the grammar doesn't require it. I do this as a means to help you see it as something that is separate to you, not something that you have or are. It will help you see it as an external thing that you can move beyond.

> IT'S AN EXPERIENCE,
> NOT A MENTAL DISORDER.

KNOWLEDGE IS ONLY GREAT WHEN YOU PUT IT INTO ACTION

I probably don't have to tell you this, but it serves as a great reminder that what you'll learn in these pages will only work if you put them into practice. During the chapters, you will come across **Superpower Activations** which are opportunities for you to stop, reflect, and do the activities I have set to help you put what you're learning into action and start changing your mindset for the better. Some will be practical strategies to put into practice in your life and business, and others will be a self exploration to unpack your current mindset to change it for the better.

Throughout the book there are multiple Superpower Activations and Resources. Head to www.christinecorcoran.com.au/impostor-book to access your free resources and enhance your learnings and experience of the book.

PREFACE

MY INNER COACH

Lastly, there are sections where I give you an insight into my "Inner Coach", this is my inner dialogue where I coach myself through my mindset blocks. My hope is that you will learn to adopt this approach too, not just accepting what your mind throws you as gospel, but rather learn to become aware of your thoughts so you can change them for the better.

Are you ready to turn the Impostor Syndrome into your superpower? Great, let's do this. First, I want to take you all the way back to August 2019 where the Impostor Syndrome almost derailed my first keynote.

Introduction

It was a rare sunny Melbourne day, and I had borrowed my sister's car to head to the conference centre. I parked close by because my heels did not allow for a long walk; the things we do to look good, right? Before I got out I took a moment in the car to reset my energy and to visualise my keynote going well one more time. I intentionally played out the entire event in my head, moment to moment, watching the audience nod along, smile, and clap at the end of my presentation with smiling faces across the crowd looking back at me. I took a snapshot in my mind and enjoyed the emotions of feeling proud and excited about how well it all went. I took a few deep breaths, gazed out the car window, and opened the door into the fresh air.

I walked into the conference centre and was greeted by an organiser I had chatted with over Zoom in preparation for this day. Her welcoming smile put me at ease as she explained that there was another speaker finishing up and there would be a 10 minute break for me to get mic'd up and ready to hit the stage.

Landing this gig—my biggest speaking keynote to date—was a long process, and it had felt like more than four months of preparation leading up to this moment. The interview and pitch process was in depth, and with every new stage I came up against the Impostor Syndrome (IS) again and again.

Australia's largest specialty fashion retailer was flying all the managers and leaders from their five iconic brands from across the country into Melbourne to be a part of a leadership conference. I was taking the stage as one of the keynote speakers to present on human behavior based leadership skills. The purpose of the keynote – and the conference at large – was to support their employees to feel seen, heard, and more integrated in the company's future goals and direction. I did not feel qualified. Up until that point, I had only spoken in front of groups of 30 to 40 people, and never a full 90 minute keynote, but I was not going to let that stop me.

INTRODUCTION

The event organiser suggested I come in and sit at a back table as the speaker was finishing up. As we walked towards the big floor-to-ceiling conference doors I could feel the anticipation building up inside me. As she opened the big door, the bright lights shone through and opened up to an enormous room, a decorated stage with a couch, a podium, and countless tables of people spreading across the room. With over 200 people giving their full attention to the stage, I immediately felt a lump rise in my throat, "Fuck, can I do this?"

At the back table, the general manager and a few other high-ranking individuals in the company introduced themselves to me. They warmly welcomed me and expressed their enthusiasm for my presentation. I smiled and nodded and thanked them for the opportunity, immediately forgetting their names because of the nerves.

As I sat there for what felt like twenty minutes—although it was probably only two—my heart race increased, my eyes darted around the room, and my breath felt shallow and fast. I couldn't concentrate on the speaker and could feel the anxiety of the moment getting to me. I excused myself to head to the bathroom; the deep breaths I was taking weren't working.

I stepped into the restrooms and walked straight up to the sink. With hands gripped to the sides of the sink I looked at myself in the mirror and said, "Get it together Christine. You've wanted to do this for years, and today is the day!"

I nervously looked around, and listened for any indication that there was anyone in the bathroom stalls and felt relief when there wasn't. I splashed some cold water on the back of my neck, took some long deep breaths and shook out my hands to try to release some of the anxious energy.

The Impostor Syndrome I knew so well was following its script: saying just the right thing to keep me in fear. I wanted to run back to the car and get the hell outta there. I looked down at my feet. They were so heavy I couldn't move. I looked at myself in the mirror again, mouth open, short shallow breaths escaping my lips, my heart beating in my ears.

I knew this was going to happen; I knew the fear would show up now. "I know how to handle this," I reassured myself out loud, trying to coax myself through the steps I so often taught to my clients. Overcoming Imposter Syndrome was part of my job, and here I was, bent over the bathroom sink minutes before my own keynote, overcome

INTRODUCTION

with it. How ironic. As I took a deep breath, I closed my eyes and navigated through my process.

I shook my hands out, releasing the built up nervous energy, put my hand on my stomach and closed my eyes. I transmuted the feeling of fear in my body to excitement and instantly felt better.

I AGAIN LOOKED AT MYSELF IN THE MIRROR AND GAVE MYSELF THE PEP TALK I NEEDED:

You are a skilled speaker. You've spoken in front of people before, you know how to do this. Get on that stage and show them you've got this. Yes, there are more people this time, but it's just a few small groups of 30 people, and you've spoken to groups of 30 before. You know what to do.

Make eye contact, connect with their energy, engage them into your presentation and follow your slides. You've practiced this for hours and hours. Your subconscious mind remembers it all, and knows exactly what to do and if you get stuck, you take a breath and ask a question of the crowd until you're back on track.

"Who are you to tell a bunch of leaders how to manage their team? You're not a leader!" the Impostor Syndrome shouted at me.

You may not be leading a team at the moment, but you've led more than a team of twenty people before and you know the challenges they face. You've also been in a conference like this before and know what it's like to sit there and listen to a speaker - so share your stories and let them know you're just like them. You get it, and you're here to give them the lessons you've learned!

Plus, you know more about human behaviour and mindset than 90% of these people in the room and your presentation is good. Teach them what you know and you'll make a positive impact. You've studied this and you know humans. Connect with the humans.

Now do your pre-speaker routine and go make yourself proud. My higher self demanded.

I adjusted my hair, touched up my lipstick, and went in to get mic'd up.

INTRODUCTION

Before going on stage, I took myself to a quiet spot, popped in my headphones and played my pre-stage songs to pump up my energy, listening and visualising the full presentation.

As I walked back into the room, someone handed me the clicker for my presentation, and after being introduced, I confidently stepped onto the stage.

I scanned the room, all eyes on me, took a few steps to the centre and asked three powerful engaging questions with people raising their hands in response to get a feel for the room. My breath was fast and shallow, I paused after each question, took a moment to slow my breathing and soothe my nerves.

Throughout the full 90 minute presentation, I remembered each part as my subconscious mind delivered it to me, taking the audience on a journey. I loved every minute. It felt energetic, engaging, and fun. Everyone stayed invested and laughed along at my many stories of what it's like managing people. I broke the audience into smaller groups for a fun exercise where I had a moment to check in with the room and the GM to ensure we were on track. I was pleased to see they were loving it.

I finished up with shares from the room and got everyone to stand as I took them through a powerful process to embody the leaders they wanted to be, finishing with a standing ovation of applause.

I didn't miss a beat, and as I stepped off that stage in my stilettos feeling proud of what I had just achieved, I felt different. With a smile from ear to ear, I took some time to chat to the organisers and wished them well for the remainder of the conference before I headed back to the car.

Sitting in the car afterwards, I sat in full gratitude for an incredible experience, replaying the 90 minutes in my head, taking the time to celebrate myself and acknowledging what worked well. The adrenaline was still running through my veins and I couldn't stop myself from smiling as I put the key in the ignition and drove off. I could now call myself a keynote speaker.

If I had let the Impostor Syndrome get to me that day, I would never have had the opportunity to prove it wrong. I would have run scared in the opposite direction and never been able to call myself a keynote speaker.

INTRODUCTION

That pesky little voice inside our heads has the best arsenal to use against us. It has the power to derail our dreams, cause us to play small and keep us stuck, doubting our abilities and talents. *If* we let it.

Rewind twelve months, the Impostor Syndrome could've derailed this whole opportunity before it even began.

You see, twelve months earlier a friend of mine who worked for the retail brand had been watching me show up online on social media sharing my message and promoting my business, and she reached out about the opportunity to speak at their conference. My initial response was a wake up call.

I was excited for the opportunity but when she asked me to send through some videos of me speaking so she could pitch me to the general manager for that year's conference, my stomach sank. I had nothing. There was nothing I could share with her that would be beneficial or would showcase my speaking skills. No speaker reel or even videos on social media that would be even remotely worthwhile. This was a blinding realisation for me. I was calling myself a speaker, yet I was not showing up as one. My friend politely explained that she couldn't put me forward without any video content to present to the GM.

They required it, which I completely understood. "Maybe next year," she'd said forlornly.

From that moment, I made it my mission to get more video footage of me speaking in preparation for the opportunity the year after. I would take this as the sign, the decision, to move through the fear of overcoming Impostor Syndrome and begin recording myself speaking. Up until that point, I had let my Imposter Syndrome talk me out of it every time, "You're not an expert, you don't know what you're talking about, everyone is going to laugh at you, judge you, and see right through you," it had nagged time and time again.

But if I was going to achieve my next level dreams, I would have to put myself out there and challenge myself to overcome that fear for good. This set off a multitude of experiences and opportunities that led me to turn the Impostor Syndrome into my superpower for growth and success.

After years of coaching women in business to overcome Impostor Syndrome, I've seen it plague even the most successful women for too long. To then see them triumph in spite of it, has encouraged me to share the tools with as many people as I can so you too can stop letting the Imposter Syndrome keep you from realising your dreams.

INTRODUCTION

It is possible to prove to yourself and others what you're not only capable of, but born to do.

So over the next few chapters I'm going to not only teach you how to overcome the fear based thought pattern that is Impostor Syndrome, but how to turn it into a tool you can use to expand yourself personally, professionally, and ultimately upgrade your experience of life.

Whether or not you have a business, you can still use these tools I share with you to rewire your brain and overcome Impostor Syndrome again and again and allow yourself to live into your fullest expression. No more hiding, no more playing small, and no more getting in your own way.

So if you're done with letting Impostor Syndrome talk you out of opportunities, expansion, and growth, then come with me.

> IT'S GOING TO BE SO SIMPLE YOU'LL WISH YOU HAD KNOWN THIS YEARS AGO.

One

WE ALL EXPERIENCE THE IMPOSTOR SYNDROME

"I STILL HAVE A LITTLE IMPOSTOR SYNDROME . . . IT DOESN'T GO AWAY, THAT FEELING THAT YOU SHOULDN'T TAKE ME THAT SERIOUSLY. WHAT DO I KNOW? I SHARE THAT WITH YOU BECAUSE WE ALL HAVE DOUBTS IN OUR ABILITIES, ABOUT OUR POWER AND WHAT THAT POWER IS."

—*Michelle Obama* FORMER FIRST LADY OF THE UNITED STATES

60% of women delay starting their own business because of Imposter Syndrome. Feeling they lack the confidence or self belief, thinking they don't deserve success despite having the necessary skills. (**NatWest Group**)

84% of entrepreneurs experience Imposter Syndrome at some stage. This feeling is particularly prevalent in the early stages of business when they are navigating uncertainties and challenges. (**EFund Business Advising**)

Up to 90% of women in leadership positions report experiencing Imposter Syndrome, including business owners, which often holds them back from taking bold steps in their ventures. (**Keepon EFund Business Advising**)

These are pretty big stats. I would go as far to say that I believe these numbers would be higher if the studies had been larger. I believe *everyone* experiences Impostor Syndrome. These stats are 100% why I felt called to write this book. Too many of us allow Impostor Syndrome to derail our dreams and cause us to play small instead of backing ourselves, believing in our abilities, and going after what we want. As things stand, the conversation of Impostor Syndrome is one of defeat. Online, in conference rooms and one-to-one, the conversation usually frames Imposter Syndrome as the reason someone cannot go after what they want, like it's an incurable disease and one they'll just have to live with, meaning their dreams are over. This just isn't the case.

Too many of my clients hold themselves back, believing the words of their Impostor Syndrome as truth until I work with them to change that. Holding on to this fixed mindset prevents them from fully living an extraordinary life because they accept Imposter Syndrome as fact rather than something they can change. They believe that because they have a thought like, 'I'm a fraud, they're going to figure it out,' that it must be true.

BECAUSE THEY THINK, 'I'M NOT GOOD ENOUGH OR QUALIFIED ENOUGH,' IT MUST BE TRUE.

I'm here to tell you: don't believe everything you think. Impostor Syndrome is not an incurable disease that cannot be overcome. It's just a series of thoughts, and thoughts can be changed.

Before we dive into changing the Impostor Syndrome into your superpower, I want you to realise the incredible power your mind can have over you. With just a thought, an unsubstantiated thought, you can give up on your dreams and think you're not worthy of them, causing you to change your life direction and give up. Crazy right?! One or two simple thoughts can be the difference between living into your fullest potential or settling for a life as mediocre as it is. Aren't your dreams important to you? If you're going to be able to stop limiting yourself and truly live to your fullest, you'll need to learn to wield the power of your mind.

So with that in mind, let's dive into our first Superpower Activation.

Superpower Activation

#1: IMPOSTOR SYNDROME EXPLORATION

Let's start with two simple questions, but before you read them, I want you to commit to really allowing your mind to explore the fullest answer to these questions. Don't rush through them. Pause, take some time to journal on them and explore the questions:

1. *What if the Impostor Syndrome I experience didn't exist?*

2. *What if I felt completely confident in myself and my skills and went after my dreams with fearless abandon? What would be possible for me?*

Take your time to truly ponder on these questions and allow your mind to wander to the possibilities. What could you achieve if you no longer suffered from Impostor Syndrome? What would life be like if you were no longer afflicted by these nasty thoughts? What possibilities would open up for you if you were no longer affected by Imposter Syndrome's arsenal of judgments and comments?

Throughout the book there are multiple Superpower Activations and Resources. Head to **www.christinecorcoran.com.au/impostor-book** for all the resources mentioned.

If you no longer let fear stop you in your tracks and instead continued to take massive action towards creating the life you dream of? Could an extraordinary life be possible for you?

I'm sure it could be. Allowing your mind to perceive a reality where this fear based thought pattern (Impostor Syndrome) no longer exists, shows you the possibilities of what life could be like. And the more attention you give that reality, the more likely you are to want to move toward it. If you really let your mind wander just now, I'm sure it conjured up miraculous experiences, possibilities, and massive action taking. You possibly saw yourself achieving everything you've ever wanted in life.

Yet you're letting some made up thoughts be the obstacle that prevent you from living your best life. You're letting them keep you stuck.

That's the power your mind has over you. Don't disregard it.

Learn to harness your mind for the better.

STEP 1 - AWARENESS

We all experience our own form of the Impostor Syndrome. If you have a brain and identify as human, you've most likely experienced Impostor Syndrome at some point in your life. If you think you haven't, you've either not stepped out of your comfort zone and done something that would expand you, or you're just not consciously aware of the thoughts of fear that are affecting your everyday behaviour.

You see, the most important step in turning the Impostor Syndrome into your superpower is first to become aware of how it shows up for you. You need to know where it's holding you back, what arsenal it uses in its defence strategies, and when it shows up for you, so you can learn to harness it.

Without awareness, our thoughts can go unchecked and undetected and our behaviour undetected, which means no change can happen. You wouldn't have picked up this book if you didn't think Impostor Syndrome was affecting you, but I wanted to bring this to your attention, because whether people are aware of it or not, Impostor Syndrome affects everyone. Being fully aware of the breadth of Imposter Syndrome is important so you don't separate successful people from yourself simply because you think you're the only one afflicted with this horrible psychological phenomenon. You're not. You are not special (well you are, but for this specific purpose, you're not different to every other person on the planet.) You're human, and if you're human, you doubt yourself, you have fearful thoughts, you hold yourself back. You likely talk yourself out of doing what you want to do because you don't believe you're good enough. You, my friend, experience Impostor Syndrome.

In the process of writing this book, I went looking for examples of people experiencing Imposter Syndrome. I have so many from my own life experience, especially in my years of growing my business and many client examples, but it's always so refreshing to find that many successful

& famously talented people also reflect on their struggles with Impostor Syndrome. Jodie Foster, Michelle Obama, Lady Gaga, and Meryl Streep are among the successful, famous people who have reflected on their struggles with Impostor Syndrome.

These prominent leaders have openly discussed the doubts and fears that have plagued them, how they have perceived themselves as impostors, despite having received awards, accolades, recognition, and approval. They continue to be affected by Imposter Syndrome. And the more I am aware of it, the more I see it on social media, and TV, especially seeing someone being interviewed.

You can see it on their faces and hear it in their responses. We all experience it. I share this with you because often people believe that if they reach the epitome of success—if they receive recognition, awards, and accolades—that they would *then* believe they were good enough, and no longer experience Imposter Syndrome. But that's just not the case. It doesn't go away, no matter how successful you are. If you're striving for greatness, if you're stepping outside your comfort zone, you're going to experience Imposter Syndrome.

WE ALL EXPERIENCE THE IMPOSTOR SYNDROME

'SOMETIMES I WAKE UP IN THE MORNING BEFORE GOING OFF TO A SHOOT, AND I THINK, I CAN'T DO THIS. I'M A FRAUD.'

—*Kate Winslet*, ACTRESS

'THERE ARE STILL DAYS WHEN I WAKE UP FEELING LIKE A FRAUD, NOT SURE I SHOULD BE WHERE I AM.'

—*Sheryl Sandberg*, FORMER COO OF META

The thing is, even when there is proof of greatness, our brains will still bring up these doubtful, pestering thoughts as a way to protect us, just in case there is danger afoot. Imposter Syndrome has nothing to do with our skills, talents, or accolades, and everything to do with our brain trying to keep us safe.

So rather than think, "the only way for me to not feel like an impostor is to have the proof of success, talent, or expert status," I want you to think about how your brain is wired and how *you* have the power to rewire the programming.

It's not the qualifications, the years of experience or awards, it's about your thought patterns and your response to those thoughts that matter.

How you think determines how you feel, and being more famous, more talented, more skilled, will not change how your brain works unless you consciously choose to change your thought patterns.

When Impostor Syndrome shows up for you (notice how I said "FOR" you? This is because it's exactly what's happening, it's showing up to protect you, to keep you safe) what does it say to you? What's its unique flavour of words that it uses to disarm you?

These are common phrases I hear from people when describing Impostor Syndrome:

+ "You don't know what you're talking about"
+ "You don't know what you're doing."
+ "There's someone better, more deserving"
+ "You're not good enough to say that/do that/ ask for that."
+ "You're not experienced enough"
+ "You're not qualified enough"
+ "You're not an expert"
+ "Who do you think you are?"

- "Who am I?"
- "I feel like a fraud."
- "I don't belong here."
- "I just got lucky, it wasn't skill."
- "I'm not an expert'
- "I'm not as good as everyone thinks I am."
- "I'm not qualified for this."
- "I'm afraid of being exposed as a fake."
- "I don't deserve this success."
- "It's only a matter of time before people realise I'm not capable."
- "I'm not smart enough for this role."
- "I must work harder to prove myself."
- "Others are more talented than I am."
- "I'm just pretending to be confident."
- "I feel like I'm deceiving others about my abilities."
- "I don't have the skills/talent everyone thinks I do."
- "I'm afraid to ask questions because it'll reveal my lack of knowledge/expertise."
- "I'm not worthy of the praise I receive."
- "I'm not a real expert, just a beginner who got lucky."
- "I'm afraid of being exposed as a phoney."
- "My success is just a fluke."
- "They're going to know you're a fraud"
- "They're going to figure it out."
- "They're going to find out I'm not as competent as they believe."

I want you to take a moment and think back to a recent time you experienced your personal flavour of Impostor Syndrome, and uncover what words it used to coax you back into your comfort zone and caused you to freeze in fear?

WHAT DID IT SAY TO YOU?

It's important that you know this, because the more awareness you have around your Imposter Syndrome, the easier it is to detect when it shows up. In order to turn Impostor Syndrome into your superpower, you must first know how and when it shows up, and what arsenal it uses against you, causing you to play small.

So what does it say? And when does it show up for you?

There are so many experiences that can activate Imposter Syndrome and I'm sure you'll continue to add more to your list, but for now, take a moment to uncover a few instances where it's shown up for you in the past and notice if there are any scenarios that are similar.

Sometimes it's when you're speaking up, putting yourself out there, promoting yourself or your business, sharing your expertise. Maybe it's when you compare yourself to other people, when you hit new milestones or when you're recognised for doing a good job? Maybe it's when you meet other talented or famous people, when you're joining new groups or even starting to learn something new?

WHEN DOES THE IMPOSTOR SYNDROME SHOW UP FOR YOU?

I remember when I first decided to start my podcast, *The Next Level Life*, back in 2017. Back then podcasts hadn't become uber popular in Australia yet and after religiously following and listening to a few of my favourite American podcasts, I knew it was something I really wanted to do. I had just come off the back of two years of study on human behaviour, coaching and neuroscience, and felt called to share my lessons and experiences on everything I was learning and the positive impact it was having on my life. I wanted more people to learn this stuff so they could live happy and fulfilled lives too. I also knew how easily I found speaking to be for me, and how sitting at home alone talking into a microphone was easier than showing my face on video on social media (I did not feel ready for that—thanks Impostor Syndrome). I knew I needed a way to get my message out there if I was ever going to get my business off the ground. A podcast felt less exposing so I decided to start there.

I mapped out an episode plan and recorded a few episodes to begin with, but when I started creating the podcast art, the thought of putting it out to everyone became real and it made me freeze in fear.

I had felt confident talking about the topics I had chosen, and had even found my first guest to interview, but now that it was becoming real, that people might actually listen to my podcast, it dawned on me that people out in the world would hear what I was saying and the Imposter Syndrome kicked in with a vengeance.

Who was I to think I could teach others about mindset? Who did I think I was, starting a podcast?

You're no expert, you don't know what you're talking about, people are going to laugh at you, they're going to see right through you and judge you. Experts are going to ridicule you and tear you down, and you'll be the laughingstock of your family and friends. Don't do this. You're going to regret it, I heard the Imposter Syndrome screaming in my ear.

I sat at my desk frozen in fear as I looked at my face on the podcast tile art I had created. None of my friends had ever started businesses, none had even listened to podcasts. This was a bad idea.

Who would want to listen to you talk about the brain and mindset? You're not a psychologist, you're not a neuroscientist. Just give up now. Stay in your job, stay in your lane and forget about this, the voice in my head continued.

I stood up and took a deep breath. I knew if I sat there any longer, my brain would talk me into giving up on myself and my business altogether, and I wasn't going to let that happen. I stepped away from my desk that day and 24 hours later I came back, grabbed an A4 sized notepad and started writing down all the reasons why I should (and must) start a podcast. I needed to convince myself it was a good idea.

It started off slow.

I should start a podcast because it's less scary than doing video and I need something to attract clients into my business.

I love to talk, and podcasting is the best way to talk until my heart's content.

I jotted these notes down, but my Imposter Syndrome still came screaming back:

"YOU'RE NOBODY. YOU DON'T DESERVE TO HAVE A PODCAST. NO ONE WILL LISTEN AND IT WILL BE A FLOP."

My inner voices battled:

Who are you not to start one? Does it really matter? At the end of the day will people really care if you started a podcast?

Well, there probably won't be many people listening to begin with, and people are obsessed with their own lives, they will not care about what I'm doing for very long. Next week they'll be caring about something else.

The reason you want to start a podcast is a legitimate reason: you want to help people, and that's worthy of following through on even if it doesn't work out.

You're educated on the topic and you know how to break things down to make it so simple and practical for people to learn from. Besides, this shit could change someone's life. It could change your own!

You have lots of experiences to share that people will find value from. Your stories could help someone change their lives. Is that not reason enough?

You've studied human behaviour, neuroscience, coaching, hypnotherapy, and neurolinguistic programming. This stuff is life changing and it needs to be shared.

You don't have to call yourself an expert, you can just share from your experience.

PLUS, you did an elective in high school on how to be a radio presenter, so podcasting will be right up your alley. Haha I guess this is kinda like radio presenting.

I then took all the mental chatter my brain had torpedoed at me and started to debate with myself:

When my brain said, **"You're no expert, you don't know what you're talking about,"** I wrote this down:

I do know what I'm talking about. I've studied this. I'm not making it up. No, I'm not an expert, but I do have value to share and I know that by sharing what I know it could help other people massively. People need to know this stuff about their brain – they're out there living their lives thinking that everything they think is true and they cannot change their thoughts or feelings, but they can. People need to know this is not the case.

To, **"People are going to laugh at you. They're going to see right through you and judge you,"** I responded:

Who cares if they do?! Like really, if they laugh at me for sharing valuable information about their brains and inner workings of what it's like to be a human, and laugh at me for sharing my experience, then let them laugh. Besides, I'll probably never know if they laughed or not — it's not likely that they'll laugh in my face, they'll do it behind my back. Will I really let fear of judgement be the reason why I don't start this podcast? NO!

"Who would want to listen to you talk about the brain and mindset, you're not a psychologist, you're not a brain surgeon/neuroscientist?"

True. But I may offer a different perspective, and I'll do everything I can to make sure I'm sharing relevant and factual information so people can implement the changes into their lives as they see fit. What I want to share is not psychology. I'm not trying to be a psychologist. I'm a coach and I can share valuable information for people to better their lives. And people will want to listen because human beings are curious, especially for getting to know themselves better.

"You don't know what you're doing."

You've gotta start somewhere. People don't become experts or become great at what they do by doing nothing.

And with that, I took a deep breath, told myself, *I'm doing it scared and that's all that matters,* and hit submit. I submitted the podcast and the episodes to Apple iTunes for review and waited.

My podcast was about to go live.

The first few episodes I posted I was merely hoping to make a positive impact on those who listened, and I knew that I could only make a difference if I published the podcast.

Fast forward seven years, over 630 episodes, over 132,000 downloads, and incredible interviews, my podcast has been the best thing I ever did for myself and for my business. I am so glad I didn't let Imposter Syndrome stop me that day.

AWARENESS BRINGS OPPORTUNITIES TO CHOOSE A NEW WAY

Now that I'm aware of the thoughts, words, and arsenal that Impostor Syndrome uses against me, I can be much more alert in future situations when those thoughts run through my mind and try to derail me. I'm no longer oblivious to the thoughts that cause me to procrastinate, freeze in fear, and avoid the thing that I've set out to do.

This awareness highlights where fear is present so you can expect it, embrace it, and learn to move through it.

You see, the Impostor Syndrome you experience cannot be the end of the road. You cannot stop when the fear thoughts show up, crawl back into your comfort zone cave, and stay there. You cannot let that be your life. When you experience the Imposter Syndrome, it's just the beginning of the road, not the stop sign. On the other side of Imposter Syndrome is everything you've ever dreamed of. Don't stop now.

Don't let a few old programmed thoughts derail your dreams.

On the other side of Impostor Syndrome are the results, outcomes, and experiences you've been craving. But these cannot eventuate without first being aware of the fear and moving through it to the other side. So the more aware of when and how the Impost Syndrome shows up, the easier it is to turn it into your superpower.

> PAY ATTENTION. NOT JUST TO
> YOUR THOUGHTS, BUT TO YOUR
> BEHAVIOUR, AS WELL.

Sometimes we don't even notice we've had any fear-based thoughts. Sometimes we find ourselves procrasta-cleaning, or doing something completely unrelated two hours later because the Impostor Syndrome has taken the wheel, and has driven us down a familiar road of activities we've done many times before because its easier and safer than feeling the fear and taking the scary, new action.

This is why bringing more awareness to your thoughts and behaviours will give you powerful insight into what's creating your current results in life or business. If you find yourself distracted with that shiny thing, or doing something unrelated to the scary thing you were about to do, there *must* have been a thought that activated fear inside you that caused you to do something else instead of the task at hand.

This happened to me recently when I had decided to pitch a podcast guest collaboration to someone I had been following on social media for years. The guest I was reaching out to has a huge following and is someone who I look up to in my industry. As fate would have it, I had booked to attend an event in the United States and it turned out I was going to be in her city for a few extra days. When I realised this, I thought to myself, *wouldn't it be amazing to interview her for the podcast?*

I felt in my gut I wanted to do this. I would have to send her a pitch. I sat on it for a few days thinking about what I would say, I mentioned it to a friend who enthusiastically encouraged me to do it, and I listened to another podcast talking about "losing every shot you don't take", and so I knew it was something I had to do. When would I ever get this opportunity again?

It's not everyday you travel 15 hours on a plane to a random city in The USA and overlap with a leader you admire immensely. I woke up one morning with the pitch in my head and immediately went to my laptop to get it down on digital paper.

I opened an email and started writing it out. I finished the first draft and then got some breakfast and a coffee before reviewing it to send.

I found her email address, added it to the email, re-read it, added a few last details, and admired it, feeling like it was a great pitch.

I then got busy with my day. Coaching session after coaching session before finally getting back to my emails.

I sat there looking at the pitch again. And before I knew it, I found myself in the living room hanging up some washing. I had vacuumed the floor, put some clothes away, and made another coffee before realising what I was actually doing.

I was avoiding sending that email.

I felt sick to my stomach. I knew I was avoiding it. Fear consumed me.

I back tracked my steps and took a moment to think about what was running through my mind before I found myself doing the washing:

What if she doesn't respond? Who are you to pitch to have her on your podcast? Your podcast is pathetic compared to hers. Your following is non-existent compared to hers, you're not good enough to even ask such a thing.

Yep, the Impostor Syndrome was kicking my ass.

So I decided to give a voice to that little fucker. I said the truth out loud, "I'm scared."

I took the coach route and imagined I was coaching myself through the fear.

I asked myself, *What are you afraid of?* And then responded to myself out loud. I know this sounds crazy, but speaking out loud to yourself is an effective tool to help you move through the fear and really uncover what's going on in your head. Plus sometimes when you say things out loud you realise how ridiculous they are and you instantly feel different about it. This is how the conversation played out:

She's going to reject me and rejection feels like shit, my self doubt exclaimed.

My Inner Coach emerged, speaking to me in a calm, practical manner, 'You're right, rejection does feel like shit. It's not nice, but you don't know she's going to reject you. There could be fifty different reasons why she may not accept this request. There are time constraints on your ask, she may be very busy the week that you're there, there are logistical reasons why she may not be able to. But no reason is a good enough reason not to ask. You'll never get a YES is if you don't ask.'

I felt defeated, but I wasn't going to let this stop me. I shifted my energy, shaking out my arms, and standing up to step into my shoes as a coach to respond.

You have nothing to offer, my inner voice retorted.

'Yes, you do,' responded my Inner Coach, 'You have a loyal and engaged audience here in Australia and you never know, she might want to expand her reach over here. Plus, all content creators need more content and you're giving her all the raw footage and recordings. She may value that.'

My podcast isn't BIG enough, I argued back again.

The Inner Coach responded calmly: 'Big enough for what? There are only a handful of podcasts worldwide that are reaching hundreds of thousands of downloads, and she likely appears as a guest on many low-ranking podcasts. Plus, your listeners are definitely her perfect audience.'

No more excuses came. My inner voice was silent, Coach had won again.

The Coach in me had one last thing to say, 'Are you willing to face a little rejection in the possibility you may get a yes? What have you got to lose?'

I re-read the email one more time, asked the universe to back me, and hit send.

Sometimes you don't know what is running through your mind until you ask it. So if you find yourself procrasta-cleaning or doing something you're not supposed to be doing, slow it down and figure out what your brain is saying to you.

Question it all. Have an argument with the fear in your head if you need to. Just like I did here. Don't let some little fear keep you playing small because just like Wayne Gretzky, the famous Canadian ice hockey player, said: "You miss 100 percent of the shots you don't take."

Two

WHAT IS IMPOSTOR SYNDROME, REALLY?

Now that we're getting more familiar with Impostor Syndrome and understanding how it shows up and what arsenal it uses, let's go a little deeper. What is Impostor Syndrome *really*?

The term "imposter syndrome" was first described in 1978 by psychologists Pauline Rose Clance and Suzanne Imes. They published their findings in the paper "The Impostor Phenomenon in High Achieving Women."

IMPOSTOR SYNDROME; NOUN;
THE PERSISTENT INABILITY TO BELIEVE THAT ONE'S SUCCESS IS DESERVED OR HAS BEEN LEGITIMATELY ACHIEVED AS A RESULT OF ONE'S OWN EFFORTS OR SKILLS.

This is a great definition, but it's a little flawed for two reasons. The two words I want you to pay attention to here are "believe" and "deserved".

BELIEVE.
What's a belief? A belief is just a thought we've thought many times. It's not the irrevocable truth. There are many truths in this world; we all have things that shape our own individual perspectives and beliefs. So if a belief is just a thought you've thought many times, that means you can change it and choose to repeat and believe a new thought instead.

DESERVED.
This one requires deeper mindset work because it's a flawed premise. What makes someone deserving? Who determines our deservedness? We do, yet society will have us believe otherwise. When we question our worthiness, we often default to not believing we're good enough to deserve the accolade or recognition we receive. So this

definition is saying that if you feel deserving, you wouldn't experience the Impostor Syndrome, but I don't believe that's the case. I think we just get better at handling the fear and reframing the doubtful thoughts that prevent us from believing in ourselves.

Our brains are programmed to doubt our merits, but this doesn't mean we cannot reprogram these negative thoughts into something more useful.

What if the reason you feel undeserving is not because you're undeserving, but because you're having a pre-programmed, disempowering thought that says so? When we take the time to identify these thoughts as just thoughts, rather than taking them as truths we are able to reprogram our subconscious mind to break free from the limitations Imposter Syndrome tries to impose upon us.

Plus the words 'persistent inability' imply that we're somehow afflicted with an inability to believe in our success. But what I find really interesting is that there are two forms of Impostor Syndrome: one that shows up when you're stepping outside your comfort zone, and doing something you've never done before, and another one where you hold a belief that you're not good enough or unworthy. When Imposter Syndrome takes hold, we accept this as a universal truth about who we are; we believe we're unworthy of what we want because there is something inherently wrong with us.

What if the reason that you exist here on this planet at this exact time means that you're worthy of everything you desire, and the only thing holding you back is your limiting thoughts telling you otherwise?

The odds of you existing right now are 1 in 400 trillion!! Let that sink in.

So if you ask me, that makes you deserving. That makes you completely worthy, and it's up to you to decide to believe in your worthiness and to view all the thoughts and beliefs you have to the contrary as just old programming that you still need to reprogram.

If that doesn't convince you, I want you to ask yourself:

WHAT MAKES SOMEONE WORTHY?

Like *really* worthy? What makes someone more worthy than another person to go after what they want? To experience what they want to experience? To be loved, to create what they want to create, to earn what they want to earn? To charge in business what they want to charge?

WHAT IS IMPOSTOR SYNDROME, REALLY?

Are there people out there in the world going after what they want who are less qualified, experienced and talented than you? Most likely. I'm confident you could name a few. So what makes them more worthy of having what they want?

WHO DETERMINES THEIR WORTHINESS?

No one determines their worthiness but themselves.

And noone determines your worthiness but you. You have to decide that you're worthy. Right here, right now. Don't let another day go by where you believe that old bullshit. You're wasting your life just going along with the programmed thoughts in your head.

Decide right now that you're going to start believing that you're worthy of everything you want.

This is pre-work to turning Impostor Syndrome into your superpower.

You have to adopt the belief that *YOU ARE WORTHY*.

You must believe that you are *ENOUGH*.

Every day we have the opportunity to believe we're worthy. It's just that our brains are following a well-programmed pattern of thoughts that lead us to believe that we're unworthy or undeserving.

If you truly want to overcome Impostor Syndrome, you have to start here - reject old beliefs, reject what society deems as worth. It's all bullshit.

Reject that old narrative and start adopting the new truth—You're worthy of everything. You're worthy of more love, life, money, success, abundance; you're more than worthy of it all.

Try it on today and see how it feels. The more you decide to believe you're worthy and to feel you're worth, the more proof will show up to demonstrate to you that you are.

Believe it now.

Otherwise, you're assigning a disempowering pattern of thought to your character that does not serve you. It's only going to keep you playing small and living a life of fear and regret.

I don't know about you, but my life is more important than that.

I don't want to waste a day sitting in fear and doubt.

Besides, it's all made up in your head anyway, so you may as well believe that you're worthy and see what happens— you might be pleasantly surprised.

But Christine, you might be asking, what if there are some things that I'm not qualified to do or experienced enough to do, isn't that a lie? There are some things that I'm not deserving of yet.

And that may be true, but what would be more useful?

Believing that you're not good enough to go after your dreams and not taking the action to get you where you want to be *or* believing that you're deserving of your dreams as you go about upskilling, learning, and growing yourself along the way?

I'm not saying you have to lie to yourself, I'm saying that you must first believe that you are inherently worthy. You were born worthy and then the world conditioned you to believe you were not.

You can choose to believe and feel worthy while in the pursuit of your dreams. While you learn more and take action towards your goals, you can feel worthy every step of the way and still want to better yourself.

So rather than give yourself a life sentence of fear and doubt, decide today that you're worthy of it all and go after what you want. Unapologetically.

The choice is yours. Continue to believe you're unworthy because of what society says or because of something that happened to you in the past, or decide today that you're already worthy.

I know which one I would choose, but you have to decide for yourself.

Three

CAUSES OF IMPOSTOR SYNDROME

The first time I applied to do a TEDx Talk, I struggled with Impostor Syndrome like crazy. I had admired Tedtalks for years, had wanted to do my own TEDx Talk, had put it on my vision board, and within a couple of weeks the announcement came out that they were looking for their next round of speakers in my city. I looked through the application process and theme and was inspired by a topic I wanted to speak on. I had a few weeks to apply so I gave myself a few days to flesh out the topic.

I woke up one night at 3 am with a complete concept of a speech. I sat bolt upright, grabbed a pen and paper (this happens often, so there's always a pen and paper on my bedside table) and scribbled down the framework for the speech.

Then I went back to sleep with a smile on my face, ready to flesh it out and get my application in the next day.

Upon waking, I reread what I'd written and felt a nervous and excited feeling deep down in my gut that always happens when I'm on the precipice of something great.

I dove into creating my application over the next few days. I reached out to a friend to run her through my idea for the speech and to get her guidance on a couple of the application questions because it wasn't a simple process. I find verbally processing helps my process. She asked me, "Have you googled how to write a Ted Talk?" Great question – no I hadn't.

I jumped off the phone and typed into Google: "How to write a Ted Talk" and hit enter.

I read through a few pages, clicked on a few links, watched a few popular Ted Talks and before I knew it, I was deep into the belly of the internet and in a spiral of self doubt. These people were experts, with lifelong experience, researchers, developers, engineers. Who did I think I was applying to speak at Tedx?

I didn't have their degrees, their education, or their experience. I was going to be laughed at, ridiculed, and the TEDx panel who judges these applications was going to immediately reject me.

This was pointless. Yep. Full self doubt Impostor spiral right here! Feeling like a total fraud, I went back to my speech plan and read over what I had written.

My speech was about women overcoming their fear of success and to do this we were going to have to overcome generations of self doubt, and years of hard wiring and programming of believing that we were not deserving of what we want. A study by Martina Horner found that women had a motive to avoid success, subconsciously fearing negative consequences for their participation or success.

I read a stat that said 66% of women have a fear of success. This blew my mind, but at the same time, I was hardly surprised. This affects women in all walks of life, from applying for a promotion, applying for a new role, going after high-level opportunities, being seen as an expert, or stepping into a position of authority.

As women, what often gets acknowledged is empathy, compassion, and heart-centred leadership, yet even then women doubt their worthiness and abilities. The only reason being is that as a society, we value masculine qualities over feminine qualities. It's not until we start to see and acknowledge our own strengths as a gender that others will start to value these qualities too.

To help women in overcoming this fear, we are going to have to overcome societal norms, gender inequality, past roles of women in the home and work, and advertising messages of low body image and high expectations of what's accepted as "beautiful" to believe that we deserve to go after what we want.

With my TEDx, I wanted to empower women to move past the fear of success and step into owning their worth and their contribution to the world, because who are they not to?

In reading my words back to myself, the thoughts of self doubt and impostor fears echoed in my mind, with the resounding response – *'Who am I to give a TEDx Talk?'* For the exact reason my speech highlighted, I felt undeserving, but my Inner Coach came back to me, "W*ho are you not to?*

Who are you not to go after what you want?

Who are you not to speak on this topic? Who are you not to empower and encourage other women? Who are you not to? You? The coach who has coached hundreds of women to overcome this exact fear. Who are you not to?

So I say the same to you. Whatever you are putting off and telling yourself you're not good enough, experienced enough, qualified enough, to do, who are you *not* to?

SERIOUSLY, WHO ARE YOU NOT TO?

Writing this book has been one of the hardest things for me to do. Writing isn't something that comes easily to me, I didn't excel in English literature at school and getting your head around writing a book is not an easy thing to do. Being disciplined enough to get my thoughts not only out of my head and onto paper, but also into a structure that makes sense, was so difficult. There were months where I would look at that little folder on my desktop and just ignore it. And then there were weeks where I felt inspired to write and empowered to share my experience no matter what my status, experience, audience, following, or qualification.

One of my favourite keynotes of all time is by Turia Pitt, bestselling author, athlete & mindset coach.

In 2011, Turia was 24 years old when she was competing in a 100km ultra marathon in the Australian outback. She encountered an out of control grassfire. Trapped by the flames, Turia sustained burns to 65% of her body, surviving against overwhelming odds, she rebuilt her life and defied every expectation placed on her.

Turia spoke to the horrific experience of surviving the marathon only having to go through a gruelling recovery period, learning to walk again through multiple surgeries, and rebuilding her life to one that she adores today with her husband and two beautiful children.

One of the key messages in her keynote, which felt like she was speaking directly to me, was: If you have something on your heart that you want to do, if you have a dream to live an extraordinary life and you are able to, then you have an obligation to pursue it. If you are able – you must. Who are you not to? And this hit home for me so deeply. It pushed all my excuses of why I couldn't to the back of my mind and the determination and clarity that came through hearing her story shifted everything.

Listening to what she went through and then what she has created and achieved in her life since then, even with all those setbacks and so many *real* reasons to give up, was a clear message to do the scary thing. It shone a light on all my bullshit excuses and called me out right there in a room of thousands of people. She was speaking right to my heart.

I remember these words time and time again, and I even recently shared them on stage at Kate Toon's CopyCon in Sydney where I spoke on all the tools I'm sharing with you today. In the end, Imposter Syndrome is just fear stopping you from achieving greatness and doing what your heart desires.

> THE MAJORITY OF THE TIME OUR EXCUSES ARE BULLSHIT ANYWAY.

Ultimately, these excuses are just stories you tell yourself to hold you back from your greatness. Some are probably real reasons to give up, but again, that's just fear talking. Shine a light now on your excuses and be radically honest with yourself: If you're able to pursue your passions - you must.

So before I break down what causes Impostor Syndrome, I want you to make a pact with yourself. A pact to go after those big scary dreams and never let the excuses that the Imposter Syndrome uses keep you stuck. Let the words of Turia ring true for you too: *If you're able - you must!*

There are many things that cause the Impostor Syndrome to surface, and the three main ones I see in the work I do coaching women in business to succeed are from a lack of belief in our skills/abilities, a lack of belief in self, and a lack of evidence from the past.

In various situations, the Imposter Syndrome can appear due to a combination of causes. Some will be about your past, some will be about the future, and some will be about the deep seated beliefs you have about yourself. Either way, only once you're aware of them can you change them.

So let's break it down.

LACK OF BELIEF IN OUR SKILLS/ABILITIES

When I got caught up in comparison looking at other Ted Talk experts, I was ultimately triggering my own doubts and fears about my skills and abilities. I doubted my ability to inspire on stage. I doubted my qualifications looking at all their degrees and years of research, and I doubted my skills as a coach, even after years of coaching 100s of women.

None of that meant that my Ted Talk wouldn't be valuable to those who listened. I got so caught up in my head about my own skills and abilities that I discounted the skills that I had.

I didn't acknowledge what I brought to the table as a speaker and as a coach. The possibility that my unique way of sharing my message would be impactful and worthwhile, didn't cross my mind.

When we doubt our skills and abilities, the first thing we tend to do is strive to learn more to feel like we're "enough". Experienced, skilled, talented, knowledgeable…you choose, whichever word precedes "enough" for you. We feel like we're lacking, so we want to add more, but that's not always necessary.

When we stay in that fear of not being enough, the Imposter Syndrome is rampant and will always keep us settling for less than we deserve. We get stuck in the fear of being judged for not being enough, or rejected. So how do we pull ourselves out of it?

First, we don't discount our own value in the process.

Let's be honest, we're not taught to believe in ourselves. We're not taught to acknowledge our skills and abilities regularly so we can support ourselves in moments of doubt. However, you can learn this, and although your parents tried their hardest, it's your job as an adult to reprogram your thinking and overcome self-doubt.

There are always going to be people who are more qualified, more talented, more skilled and more capable than you, but that does not mean you should downplay your abilities. It does mean that you should still throw your hat in the ring and give it a go, because the best way to strengthen your belief in your skills and abilities is to put them to good use. Prove to yourself that you're capable in order to believe in yourself more.

It's not just in the learning of the knowledge that makes someone an expert, it's in the application of their skills and abilities, too.

Comparison is another sure way to derail our belief in our skills and abilities. When comparing yourself to others and you come across someone more qualified or experienced than you, do you put them on a pedestal in your mind? Do you make yourself smaller, or less than, and see them as better than you? Or do you just see them as another human doing their thing?

We need to learn to compare intelligently. As soon as we put someone on a pedestal, we put them above us and we place ourselves below, which implies we are less than. When we deem someone else to be better than us, we discount our own skills and abilities, and ultimately our own value. It's a natural response that can happen when we compare ourselves, so it's up to us to learn to interrupt this negative spiral and make sure we pull them down off the pedestal (theoretically) because they are human just like you and me. Remember to lift yourself up so you're an equal human being doing great things, irrespective of the other person.

Rather than looking at others and discounting our own value, we must learn to acknowledge the other persons qualities and skills, knowing that they too are skills we'd like to develop and maybe there is something we can learn from observing them.

This can also happen when you're first sharing something new to the world, where you have no proof yet that it's going to work. I remember a client in one of my masterminds got so bogged down with Impostor Syndrome when she was writing her sales page for her new program, and when it got to the part about what results the potential clients could expect, she froze. She didn't know. She wasn't sure what to promise because it was the first time running the program. Immediately she found herself doubting her skills and abilities, thinking, "Who am I to teach this? What if I can't deliver on what I say? What if it doesn't work?

And just like I had refocused my attention on the audience for my Ted Talk application, I told her to focus on her dream clients, and I asked her to write down ten reasons why and how she was able to help them. Once she did this, she felt much more confident in being able to sell her program because she realised she did have the skills and abilities to help them. She only needed to be two steps ahead of the people she needed to help, and she had the skills and abilities to be able to help them. You don't have to be the *best* to help the people you want to help, you just have to believe in your skill to be able to help them where they're at.

Other areas this can show up is when you're going after opportunities: taking on new roles in business or corporate careers like a new leadership role, going for a promotion, being nominated for an award, applying for a grant, or even pitching for funding. In each case, we generally have to boast about skills, abilities, and qualifications. It feels daunting, leading us to feel like we're not enough.

Remember it's probably not true. Just your brain trying to protect you.

LACK OF SELF BELIEF

When we have a fundamental lack of belief in ourselves, as individuals, we can also sabotage our success by listening to the Impostor Syndrome, because we already believe we're not good enough.

It's not true, you are enough. You've just gotten really good at believing you're not.

We walk around this world with a concept of who we are and who we're not. This identity is made up of all your past experiences, memories, education, upbringing, culture, religion, and with all that, you have built a concept of who you believe you are.

Our self-belief determines how we perceive our talents and capabilities, influencing our response to new situations and opportunities. Unfortunately, life often fails to teach us to cultivate strong self-belief. Society often teaches us to doubt and judge ourselves, making it hard to believe in ourselves, but it's crucial for a happy and successful life.

When we have a fundamental lack of self belief, we believe we're not good enough. We question our ability to handle things, and we question if we're enough. We only tell ourselves we're not because we haven't developed a strong sense of self.

This is a perfect breeding ground for Impostor Syndrome and often when partnered with a lack of confidence, it can become a pattern of self talk that can track all the way back to adolescence or childhood. Maybe you weren't celebrated for your skills and abilities as a student, or maybe you were not allowed to make mistakes as kids, or your efforts weren't good enough in the eyes of the people you looked up to. Either way, you adopted the belief that you weren't good enough.

As an adult now, it's important that you separate the past from the present and start attributing your capabilities to who you are as a person. The results and outcomes you've created in your life so far wouldn't have been possible if you weren't capable enough to make them happen. Look at the facts.

We don't take time to stop and take stock of our lives and who we have become over the years. We don't ask powerful questions like, *who am I really?*

We attach labels of wife, mother, business owner, sister, qualification title etc, and see that as who we are, but we're so much more than that.

CAUSES OF IMPOSTOR SYNDROME

If you dropped all the labels, how would you describe yourself?

WHO ARE YOU?

You, my gorgeous human, are a bunch of unique qualities that make you who you are.

You are kind, generous, funny, resilient, caring, loving, determined, and tenacious.

Once you know who you are beyond the labels, the biggest underlying factor of developing a strong sense of self and self belief is cultivating self trust. It's the essential part to believe in yourself and most of us haven't developed our self trust. Or maybe we've become untrustworthy to ourselves, going against our own inner knowing time and time again.

We've gone against our own values, we've put everyone else first, we've given up on ourselves, we've talked shit about ourselves, and judged ourselves. We haven't had our own backs, and that fosters distrust.

Self trust is built over time. When you honour your word with yourself, meaning you do what you say you're going to do, especially when it comes to your own needs you strengthen your self worth and build trust with yourself.

If you want to be able to believe in yourself more, you've got to create a deep sense of self trust and learn to back yourself again and again. To become your own cheerleader and always do what you say you're going to do and the trust you create will make you unshakeable.

When we don't do what we say we're going to do (especially when it comes to our own needs) we create a relationship with ourselves where we can't be trusted, and you can't back someone you can't trust.

You have to believe you're capable. When you honour your word with yourself by doing the things you say you're going to do, you develop a deep sense of self trust and someone who can trust themselves becomes unstoppable.

When you develop this kind of relationship with yourself, you're able to acknowledge your own inner qualities, your skills and abilities and your talents, and when you do that, you believe you're capable of so much more. Capable of being able to take action, do big scary things, and honour yourself in the process, because you have your own back. It's the cornerstone of confidence, resilience, and self worth.

If you find it hard to attribute your success to who you as a person, don't worry, you're not alone and you're not doomed. You can train yourself to do this. It's common for most people to find this task extremely difficult and unfamiliar at the beginning. Especially if you were brought up in a household where your flaws or mistakes were pointed out instead of your strengths. Or if you learned to outsource your self worth, always looking to others for the answers and for approval. If you've done this, you've basically trained yourself that trusting yourself isn't possible, but it is, and it's required for overcoming Impostor Syndrome.

It is so important you learn to do this for yourself because if you don't retrain this internal response, you'll never feel deserving of the things you actually do accomplish. So if you're waiting to feel successful, accomplished, and proud of yourself, you have to train yourself to know how to feel that way.

Do you need to build self trust? Do you have your own back?

Keep yourself accountable to building self trust by writing down the things that are important to you, and the things you're going to do to honour your word with yourself.

And be sure to pay attention to the thoughts or things you say. If you say you're going to do something, but deep down you know you're not going to do it, learn to practise honesty with yourself - don't say it if you know you're not going to do it, that's just going to build more distrust. Only say what you are going to do and then do it. Start small and you'll notice you'll start to back yourself more and feel accomplished in the process.

When I stopped saying things to myself that I knew I wasn't going to do, and was truly honest with myself, I was able to develop the discipline to honour my word with myself with the things that were important to me, knowing that if I said I was going to do it, I did it no matter what. I became obsessed with it. My confidence grew and I no longer betrayed myself. That's when my self belief started to skyrocket.

Your word with yourself is everything. Its your self integrity. It's your relationship with yourself that matters most, as you've got you for the rest of your life, and if you don't honour your own word with yourself, you'll never trust or believe in yourself. It's vital if you want to feel confident, take scary action and do big things.

LACK OF EVIDENCE FROM THE PAST/ FEAR OF THE UNKNOWN

Another cause of Imposter Syndrome is when we have a lack of proof from the past that we're going to be safe as we step into doing something we've never done before. Our brain is a magnificent and efficient machine that works so fast to compare our current situation with the past, ultimately looking for similarities between experiences to determine if we're going to be safe.

Your brain stores every experience in your memory bank alongside the emotions you felt in relation to that experience, and like the big filing cabinet scene in the Pixar movie, *Soul*, where Jerry is looking for the soul memory, your brain stores and remembers everything and compares that evidence to the present moment.

So when we're stepping outside our comfort zone, doing something we've never done before, in a millisecond, the brain scans the past for anything familiar. If there is nothing similar, our brain can deem the present situation to be new and dangerous, activating Impostor Syndrome to keep you safe. This little protection mechanism is usually very effective, but the biggest realisation is that if you want to experience new things and live a fulfilled life, you're going to have to do things you've never done before and this little fear response/protection mechanism is just a normal part of the process that you needant be afraid of. You must remind yourself that just because you've never done it before does not mean it's dangerous, it's just new. Ultimately, everything in the future is unknown, but your brain is always looking for the evidence of your past to determine your safety and looks for certainty of that safety in every possible outcome. It's natural that when there is no evidence from the past, Impostor Syndrome arises to protect you from a new unknown.

Four

OTHER SYMPTOMS OF IMPOSTOR SYNDROME

"NOW WHEN I RECEIVE RECOGNITION FOR MY ACTING, I FEEL INCREDIBLY UNCOMFORTABLE. I TEND TO TURN IN ON MYSELF. I FEEL LIKE AN IMPOSTER . . . ANY MOMENT, SOMEONE'S GOING TO FIND OUT I'M A TOTAL FRAUD, AND THAT I DON'T DESERVE ANY OF WHAT I'VE ACHIEVED."

—*Emma Watson*, ACTRESS

QUESTIONING YOUR WORTHINESS EVEN WHEN YOU HAVE THE EXPERIENCE OR QUALIFICATIONS

Emma Watson, known most prominently for her role in Harry Potter and as an activist of various causes, has publicly admitted to falling into the trap of Imposter Syndrome. In an interview with Vogue and another with Rookie Mag in 2013, she shared how she feels when people offer her praise for her acting:

Has there been a time in the past where you had the talent, qualifications, or skills that made it possible to achieve something, and you still found it hard to feel like you deserved the recognition? The facts tell you logically that you deserve it, but there's something deep inside that makes it hard to accept.

This happens when we don't take the time to attribute our accomplishments, achievements, and results to who we are as people. We disregard them because we have an underlying belief that we're not good enough. This is that pesky 'persistent inability to believe in one's success' showing up with gusto.

You do deserve the recognition, and it's time to override that little inner chatter and learn to acknowledge yourself first. More on how to do this soon when we learn how to attribute accomplishments to your self worth and upgrade your identity.

THINKING YOU'RE LUCKY WHEN YOU ACHIEVE SOMETHING

You're not lucky. Can we just stop saying that?

Who do you know that has achieved something great, that was *only* lucky? There may have been some luck or privilege involved, but it's not the only contributing factor. When you say you were lucky, you're disregarding the action you took and the personal qualities that made that result possible. I'm going to teach you how to stop doing this because I want you to own your success. Unapologetically.

INABILITY TO CELEBRATE YOUR WINS

Do you get caught up going after the next thing, and the next thing? Never feeling like you're getting anywhere and never feeling like you've achieved anything great? This is probably because you haven't celebrated your wins along the way, big and small, most importantly small. Would it be true to say that most of the time when you get to your goal, or you've achieved something, it doesn't feel worthy enough of recognition? It never feels like "enough"? This is

Impostor Syndrome too! If you're unable to celebrate the small wins, the big wins will also never feel like enough.

The goal posts are always moving (especially in business and success), so if you're not celebrating and attributing your results and accomplishments to who you are as a person, and allowing yourself to feel good during the process, you'll never feel good enough.

YOU'LL ALWAYS BE STRIVING FOR MORE, NEVER GETTING TO THE END.

I remember when I first hit six figures in my business, it was a random Tuesday when I did my accounts and realised I had surpassed the milestone a week earlier. Sitting at my desk, writing emails for the week ahead I remember feeling excited that I had hit the milestone I had been working to for so long. And twenty minutes later, I was back writing those emails and working on other bits and pieces, like nothing had happened. It wasn't until I sat down to do my CEO ritual that Sunday, reflecting on the week that had just passed, and took the time to properly celebrate and acknowledge myself for achieving the milestone, that I was able to fully experience the joy of achieving it. If we don't stop, we can so easily get caught in the rat race of more and the hustle of life never truly feeling fulfilled. If you don't practise the positive emotions of joy, excitement, pride, exhilaration, euphoria, (all the emotions you think you'll feel when you achieve your milestones) you'll not really be able to tap into the emotion fully and you'll just go back to your everyday practiced emotions, which are usually negative ones like fear, guilt, anger, frustration and anxiety.

Where the actual celebration goes beyond the superficial celebration, and becomes strong self belief is when you realise the true inner qualities that made it possible for you to achieve a goal. Stop waiting to achieve the *big* goals in order to celebrate and start practising the positive emotions you want to feel when achieving the small ones. Stop and take stock regularly and be proud of your progress. How else will you enjoy the journey?

All of these symptoms are Impostor Syndrome stopping you from owning your worth and believing in yourself and your inevitable success. It wants you to disregard your skills, abilities, and self belief, because it wants you to play small where it's safe, certain, and comfortable.

Now that we know the causes of Impostor Syndrome, we can be aware of them, expect them and be ready to face them.

You know you're here for more, and for more to happen you are going to have to step outside your comfort zone again and again which means you're going to have to change your response to fear and turn the Imposter Syndrome into your superpower!

ARE YOU READY TO LEARN HOW?
LET'S DO THIS.

HOW TO TURN IMPOSTER SYNDROME INTO YOUR

Superpower

STEP ONE

Expect It

Five

ARIZONA

I stood in the courtyard of a luxury resort conference room with about 70+ high-level entrepreneurs mingling and meeting each other for the first time. I was standing with two other seemingly lovely women, not fully present in the conversation. I was feeling super self conscious of how I appeared to others. My eyes darted around from person to person, thinking about whether I was going to fit in here. Was what I was wearing appropriate? Did I stick out like a sore thumb? Would anyone find out that I did not belong here, an Aussie trying to fit in, in the entrepreneurial world of the United States? I had flown 14 hours to Los Angeles and then a short flight over to Phoenix to be at this event, and I was feeling very out of my depth.

The Impostor Syndrome was on hyper drive and I could feel the anxiety rising in my chest. I was breathing fast and my palms were sweating. I smiled and hugged, chatted and answered the question, "You flew all the way here from Australia?" as my accent was very obviously not from America. "Yep." I nervously laughed it off while in my head I was thinking, *Had this all been a big mistake? Am I crazy stupid for making this trip? Would they all laugh me out of the room?*

I took some deep breaths, letting my longer exhale calm my nervous system and reminded myself that it was going to be ok. *They're just people, they're just people, they're just like me*, I repeated to myself. *I'm sure there are many other people standing around here having the same thoughts and doubts. There has to be.*

I looked around and noticed some people who I had admired online from afar. Some had been guest speakers at events I had attended online, and coaches I had connected with on Instagram, and quickly the inner chatter of the Impostor Syndrome I was experiencing got louder again in my head.

It all felt like a blur. I was given my name tag, finding it hard to say my name out loud, dry mouth taking over. I made my way into the room and found my seat, grabbed a drink of water and again took some deep breaths to remind myself that it was going to be OK. I pushed the chatter out of my head and started talking with someone I had met online years before as part of another mastermind, so thankful I knew someone. I had only seen her in the Zoom room but had never spoken directly to her before, and as she shared a recent win in her business it was visible that she was just as nervous as I was. After a moment of her speaking, she looked around the room, back to me and apologised for monopolising my time, to which I realised was a response to my nervous eye scanning of the room. I took a deep breath and apologised, saying "I'm so sorry, I'm really nervous. You're not keeping me from anyone, I want to hear about what's been happening for you and your business. Please continue." She smiled and we continued chatting.

The nerves slowly started to calm down and then the event kicked off with the hosts walking into the room. I was singled out for the person who had traveled the furthest and I again felt myself shrinking, questioning if this was the dumbest thing I had ever done, and whether I was even successful enough to be in this room. Who was I to think I belonged here?

It wasn't until we broke out into smaller groups and did some masterminding sessions that I started to feel more at ease. I got to know more people in the room, and when I heard them sharing their challenges and business problems, I realised they were just like me. I was able to share my experience to help others with some advice, I started to feel like I belonged.

It's a deeply human trait to want to feel like we belong everywhere we find ourselves. Based on my perceptions of other people's level of success and accomplishment in that room, I felt like I didn't belong. I felt out of my depth, not good enough, not successful or knowledgeable enough to be there, but I had to take a moment to acknowledge what I brought to the table too and to not discount my own abilities before even knowing anything about the other people in the room.

I could've let the Imposter Syndrome take that day over and not contribute to the conversations and masterminding sessions that I had paid a lot of money to be a part of. I decided in that moment that I wasn't going to let some little fear keep me from what I was there to do. I knew better. Most coaches, books, and experts talk about overcoming the Imposter Syndrome, but Imposter Syndrome isn't something to overcome, it's something we experience, especially when we're stepping outside our comfort zone, and I knew it was going to show up for me by attending this event. I was expecting it.

Rewind three months earlier, I had come to realise that I had gotten comfortable in my business. I'd pushed hard to get beyond six figures and now I had consistent income and a consistent stream of new clients coming to me. The year so far had been reasonably smooth but I had a moment where I realised I had stopped striving, I was too comfortable.

I was presenting a workshop on Impostor Syndrome to an online group of entrepreneurs and in my mind as I was encouraging them all to get out of their comfort zone and do *scary things*, I realised *I* hadn't done anything challenging recently. After that session, I sat down and reviewed my goals - they were basic and boring. There was nothing there I was excited about.

So I asked myself - what would be exciting? What would make me feel the fear? What would induce Impostor Syndrome and cause me to grow?

I wrote down a few things and I could feel the excitement start to rise. It was time to shake things up. The next day

I got an email from a past mentors sharing about a new event they were hosting in Arizona in a few months. I closed my eyes and pictured myself attending that event and quickly the Impostor Syndrome kicked in. I knew I had to be there, even though it seemed illogical, expensive, and I did not feel ready or successful enough to attend. I decided it was something I needed to do to ask more of myself, to level up my identity by surrounding myself with other successful people and to challenge myself to grow.

We're always going to experience Impostor Syndrome when we're doing something we've never done before as it's a fear based thought pattern. When you're out of your depth it shows up. It never fully goes away, especially if you've chosen a life of growth and expansion. If you are someone who wants to reach your fullest potential then you're most likely going to be someone who pursues growth and Imposter Syndrome is a part of that growth journey.

It's inevitable that Imposter Syndrome will show up to keep you safe, so stop thinking you'll ever *overcome* it, because you shouldn't want to. It's not the villain in the story, it's not the boogeyman. The Imposter Syndrome you experience is a part of you, it's a fear response. It's your brain's way of keeping you safe, calling you back into your comfort zone where you have certainty and safety of knowing the outcome. The past versions of yourself are trying to protect you from pain, embarrassment, and uncomfortable experiences by avoiding new things that may result in judgement, failure, or rejection. And deep down, none of us want to experience those things. At the same time, this Imposter Syndrome means that growth is coming.

So let's face it: Imposter Syndrome and growth are a packaged deal. If you say you want more and that you value growth, then you have to be willing to face Impostor Syndrome. Expect it.

Six

OUR RELATIONSHIP WITH FEAR

GROWTH = FEAR = OVERCOMING FEAR = GROWTH

The reason why I signed up to attend that event in the US was because I had realised I was getting too comfortable. I had been going through the motions in my business and felt like each day was looking the same - I had stopped growing. I needed something to take things to the next level and for me to feel like I was being challenged and growing again. I was bored in my comfort zone and something had to change. Ever felt like that?

Not only was the investment big and scary, but the thought of being in that room caused me to raise my standards of how I saw myself, what I expected from myself, and how I looked at my business. So, when this opportunity came up, although it felt scary, I knew it was something I had to do.

From the moment of processing the payment on that sign-up page, I knew this would activate the Imposter Syndrome; I knew it would cause me to grow. Although I was scared out of my wits, I was willing to put my money where my mouth was.

You see, if you want to grow, you're going to have to get comfortable with being uncomfortable, which means you're going to have to have a good relationship with fear, one that doesn't cause you to stay frozen and avoid doing the big scary things.

To create next level growth, you have to do the things that scare you and changing your relationship with fear has to come first before we turn Imposter Syndrome into your superpower.

Most people live their life on autopilot. Responding to the world around them the same way, going about their routines of comfortable action and living life in the safe zone week in, week out.

But not you, as I'm sure. If you've picked up this book, you're most likely wanting a bigger life. You want more. You want to expand and reach your fullest potential. You most likely value growth and for you to grow, you know you need to step out of your comfort zone, embrace fear, and do things that make you feel uncomfortable.

So let's talk about your comfort zone.

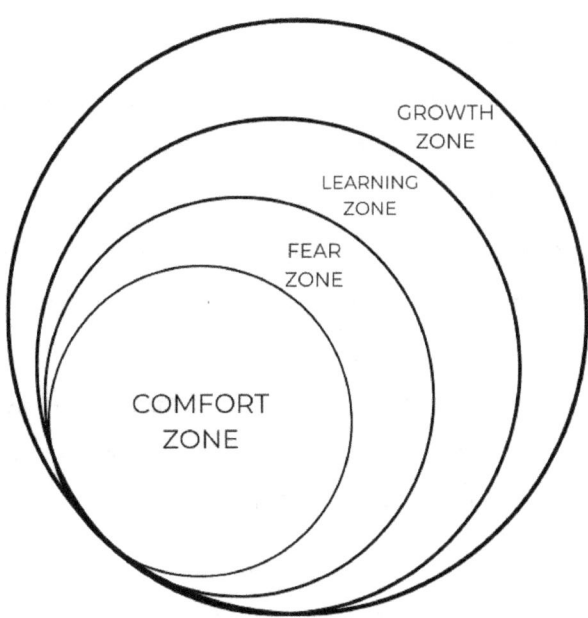

Source: PositivePsychology.com Toolkit – *'Leaving The Comfort Zone'*

COMFORT ZONE = FEAR ZONE = LEARNING ZONE = GROWTH ZONE

Your comfort zone consists of everything you've learned, developed, and become skilled at in your life, whether that be actual skills, behaviours, ways to respond to situations, and experiences you've had. This includes everything you've been told, all the things you've tried, failed, and succeeded at that exist inside your comfort zone. Think of your comfort zone like a filing cabinet or a bank, and every time you repeat a behaviour you're adding to the filing cabinet of proof, to the evidence your brain has of circumstances it can be certain of. Your brain then determines that behaviour/experience as comfortable, therefore safe.

Your comfort zone is most likely where you feel the most confident because you've repeated these behaviours time and time again, become super competent at them, and they've now become your default. Your brain deems these behaviours to be safe because you've repeated them enough times your brain is 99% certain of the outcome.

When you step outside your comfort zone, you're creating a new unpredictable scenario, and with that comes danger.

There is a new level of uncertainty. When you step out of your comfort zone, you're stepping into your fear zone.

A lot of people don't like to step outside their comfort zone because they don't want to feel uncomfortable. They've become slaves to their emotions. They fear being seen as a beginner and find it hard to put themselves back at the beginning stage again because it's uncomfortable. This is the first hurdle you have to overcome, you must first be OK with making mistakes and getting it wrong in order to learn. You cannot grow without making mistakes or being open to try by stepping through the fear zone into the learning zone.

> YOU HAVE TO BE OK WITH
> BEING A BEGINNER.

Once you've moved through the fear zone, and you're OK with being in the learning zone, you must attempt to put your knowledge into action. It's here where you step into the growth zone. We can only step into the growth zone if we're willing to move through the fear and learning zones, feeling the fear and making the move anyway. Putting what you know into action in new situations creates new evidence that you can in fact do things that you've never done before. When you put your new skills into practice enough times you go from a beginner to a skilled operator, who is competent which gives you the confidence to do it again and again.

The more you do these actions, the more you become capable, and the more confident you become and then it becomes less scary. And you have, in fact, grown. You've developed a new skill and it's now part of who you are. The more you repeat that behaviour, the easier it gets and soon you become comfortable doing it. Now you're all of a sudden back in your comfort zone.

A lot of people just stay in the learning zone never knowing what they're capable of because they don't have the courage to step through to the growth zone and put what they know into action. You know these people, the 'gonna' people: "I'm gonna do this, but I need to learn a little more first." They sign up for the next course and the next course, feeling like they don't know enough yet, waiting to feel confident before they take the action. They're getting ready to be ready. They're not willing to risk making a mistake. They're not willing to be beginners, or to feel uncomfortable. They have to know the outcome of all the worst case scenarios before they'll take the next step, and even then, they still won't take the leap. These people are usually the most knowledgeable people in the room, but they stay stuck because they're not willing to feel the fear and take the scary action.

The only way for you to become confident and no longer feel scared to try something new is to repeat that same scary action enough times until you become competent. Without competency, you cannot be confident. Most successful people don't become successful because they have no fear, they become confident and successful because they're willing to feel the fear and do it anyway. They trust, or know, that beyond that fearful step is their ability to experience and learn something new in order to become more competent and to have grown beyond their previous capabilities.

How willing are you to be uncomfortable? How willing are you to be a beginner and make a mistake? Your ability to feel the fear and take the action anyway can be the difference between moving beyond this first step and allowing yourself to learn, or choosing to stay stuck.

Resistance to taking that next step is also fear showing up to protect you. It's not always big neon signs and the feeling of terror taking over, it's the little resistances day to day, to taking the next step which you have to be aware of as well.

To do this, you must be aware of your fear response. The more aware of your fear response the easier it is to move through the fear, into the learning zone and then into the growth zone.

We need to learn to expect fear when we take action and learn to understand the response we experience so we can transmute it into something more useful.

Do you know what your fear response is?

You may have heard of the freeze, fight, or fly response?

Let's explore your default fear response so you can learn to understand it and change your relationship with fear for the better.

Throughout the book there are multiple Superpower Activations and Resources - Head to www.christinecorcoran.com.au/impostor-book for all the resources mentioned.

Superpower Activation
#2: FEAR AND RESISTANCE

Take a moment to think back to the last three times you experienced fear or resistance to taking an action. Write each moment down on a notepad and replay each scenario separately in your head, writing down how you reacted to each of these situations. Ideally we want to see what the default response is, so looking at multiple scenarios will give us a more accurate view.

With each situation, ask yourself these questions:
+ What happened?
+ If you slow the process down, what activated the fear response?
+ What did you find yourself doing or not doing?
+ How did you feel?
+ What thoughts did you have?

Reflecting on all three, which one was your default? Did you freeze, run away (fly), or get defensive (fight)? Let's break down each one for clarity.

Seven

THE THREE FEAR RESPONSES

"NOTHING IN LIFE IS TO BE FEARED, IT IS ONLY TO BE UNDERSTOOD. NOW IS THE TIME TO UNDERSTAND MORE, SO THAT WE MAY FEAR LESS."

—Marie Curie

Fear shows up in many ways and the more you get to know the unique ways fear shows up in your life the more control you'll have over the outcomes you create and whether you let fear run your life. The most interesting fears to uncover are not the big scary fears of potential worse case scenarios that we think will hold us back, but actually the little fears that keep us stuck on the daily. Fear often shows up as resistance to taking an action and if we can learn to catch those little fears we can transform our lives incredibly.

So what's your fear response?

Reflecting on those past three experiences from the above Superpower Activation, which one was your common response?

FREEZE

The freeze response is just that: freezing in place. This is the "wait and see" response. You find yourself frozen in place and cannot take action. You find yourself spinning your wheels, staying focused on the problem and nothing else.

FIGHT

When we have a fight response, we get defensive, frustrated, and angry at a situation. We find ourselves wishing it was different, and we get defiant in our reaction. We sometimes can blame others, the world or the situation as to why we cannot take action instead of seeing it as fear. In fight mode, we may get caught up in the frustration of wanting things to be different. Despite this desire for a different outcome, we don't actually do anything. Ultimately, fear shows up as being scared of something not working out, going wrong, or even *being* wrong.

FLY

Do you find yourself running away from fear? Doing anything but facing it? Find yourself distracting yourself with other things, getting busy with something new as if the original task wasn't a priority? Maybe you procrastinate and find yourself cleaning? When we fly away from fear, we get caught up in something new, or get completely distracted by something different.

When I first started to learn about fear responses, I never really resonated with the three responses. It wasn't until the FIGHT response was described as a defensive reaction that I realised my fear response was FIGHT. I found myself getting angry at myself, at the situation at hand, and finding anyone that would listen to justify why I was angry. It kept me stuck in my fight response, instead of realising my true emotion: FEAR.

I was frustrated. I found myself angry that it wouldn't work out, angry I would look stupid, or I would fail. It wasn't anger. It was fear presenting as anger. Now I can identify it for what it is: fear. Having this ability to identify fear allows me to address it and transmute that fear into something much more useful when it arises.

We commonly have a consistent default response, yet we can experience all three. Which one is your most common response?

Eight
TRANSMUTE THE FEAR

Once we're aware of our fear response, we're becoming more aware of how fear shows up in our lives. And the most profound work you can do is to learn how to transmute that feeling of fear into an emotion that's much more useful. What do I mean by useful? Let me explain.

You see our emotions drive all of our behaviour, all of them. There is never a time where a behaviour is not driven by an emotion which has either been a habitable programmed emotion or an emotional response to a thought you had. If you're feeling fear and it's causing you to freeze, fight, or fly instead of addressing the problem, then it's not a useful emotion. Fear is only useful when you're in true danger.

We want to learn to transmute that fear into a more useful emotion that may drive a different behaviour, like curiosity or inspiration which then may lead to a more useful action. Many people walk around this earth, thinking they have no control over their emotions; they feel trapped by them, out of control, and as though they lack the ability to manage their emotions. In these instances, they are just reacting, not responding with a clear head. But this is where we can become more in control of our lives, by learning to proactively choose how we want to feel. Instead of just reacting and choosing how we want to respond. It's about taking full responsibility for how you want to feel and your own life experience.

For instance, wouldn't you rather feel excited than fearful?

Wouldn't you rather be interested than sceptical? Curious, rather than trapped?

Excitement and fear are, in fact, closely intertwined in the brain. They share the same physiological reactions: the adrenaline that courses through the body when a person is scared is the same as when they are excited.

We respond to how we feel, yes, but we also have thoughts that activate emotions. The body reacts to our emotions, and our emotions react to our thoughts. The only difference being how your mind interprets the experience.

Can you remember back to a time in the past when you felt excited?

Think of one now and remember how your body responded.

Do you remember feeling your heart-rate increase? Maybe you were breathing faster, felt your hands clam up?

What about when you've felt fearful? Did your heart rate increase? Get clammy hands and start breathing faster? Maybe you forgot to breathe. Or, you felt butterflies in your stomach and you became hyper aware of your surroundings. Your pupils also dilate to help you focus on the potential danger. The adrenaline kicks in and so does the cortisol to get the body ready to run or fight.

The blood rushes from your brain to your extremities to prepare your muscles to run, you start breathing faster to get more oxygen into your lungs, and your heart rate increases to pump that blood around your body.

The only difference between feeling fear and excitement is the way you breathe. When you're in a fear response, you either hold your breath in freeze mode or you breathe shallow, short breaths in the top part of your chest. When you're excited, you breathe more fully, deeper and from the diaphragm.

So while you still have the clammy hands, the butterflies in your stomach, and a racing heart, fear causes you to breathe in a different way than excitement.

Now the cool part is that because you're human, you have the ability to interpret these sensations in your body and transmute them into whatever you decide.

You can react and choose to feel fear or you can interpret it as excitement instead, remember to breathe and transmute it to excitement.

The meaning you place on the sensation will determine what happens next.

You could feel fearful as you step out onto that stage to speak, or you could choose to feel excited. You could acknowledge that you're nervous and interpret that feeling as an indication that it's something you care about, or you could tell yourself you're terrified and turn the fear up a notch and go into full fight or flight response.

YOU DECIDE.

Most people just *react* instead of choosing *how* they want to interpret the emotion and bodily sensations.

You can choose to feel any emotion you decide to. It's as simple as imagining something that will generate the feeling you seek, or remembering a time when you felt that feeling, and then activate it in your body.

I can call in what calm feels like and I am able to tell my body that it's safe. I practiced this in Arizona when I sought to calm my nerves at the event. By focusing on the person I was speaking to upon arriving at the event, rather than the fear thoughts in my head, I was able to use my breath to calm myself. I decided to remind myself why I was there so I could experience the event the way I wanted to experience it, rather than getting caught up in the stress.

Stepping back to recenter and redirect my emotions allowed me to actually enjoy the day. For months leading up to the event, I had been so excited to get into that room; I wasn't going to let fear stop me from enjoying it.

You get to choose. Don't let your emotions get the better of you, decide to transmute them to more useful emotions.

Fear was not serving me in that room. Feeling scared, I wasn't able to focus. I wasn't able to be present, or be my normal bubbly self. I was self-sabotaging, and I didn't want that. Calming my nerves with my breath, transmuting it into courage and excitement was much more useful in the moment and it allowed me to show up as my best self, engage with those who I interacted with, and, most importantly, enjoy myself.

Transmuting your emotions begins with how you respond and interpret them. Our emotional vocabulary can sometimes be very limited, leaving us with four to five words to describe how we feel on a day-to-day, month-to-month basis. The English language has more words to describe negative emotions than we do positive ones. Think about it, when someone asks how you are, how often do you describe yourself as good, fine, not bad? Why not choose great, fantastic, relaxed or content? How you describe your experience will impact how you feel.

Your body is also responding to how you interpret your feelings every day. When you say you're tired, your brain scans your body to see how and where you feel tired and brings awareness to that area, registering more tiredness. Our body and brain work together to live in accordance with our identity. So if you say you're tired, your brain will look for the proof. Try it. Say out loud: "I feel tired."

Pay attention to what happens afterwards. Does your body slump, do you breathe more shallowly, do you notice tired muscles, aches, and pains?

When you say you feel energised, your body responds by looking for energy, possibly breathing in deeply and standing up tall and getting ready to produce more energy. Your body is always listening and responding, and what you tell it matters, especially when using the words "I AM."

Whatever words you use after "I AM" become part of your identity.

So when we have a limited vocabulary to describe how we're feeling, it makes it hard to respond in new sensations unless we consciously choose to expand our vocabulary and explore how we *truly feel*. Want to feel happier? Start training yourself to feel happier by practicing the feeling of happiness. When you smile for more than a minute, your body responds by tricking yourself into thinking you're happy. Science has shown that by smiling, you activate a chemical response in the brain to produce more dopamine and serotonin, the feel good hormones which can lift your mood, lower stress, and boost your immune system. Whether you started off feeling happy or not, your body responds to the physicality of the smile.

What's your range of emotions? On a month-to-month basis, how many emotions do you feel? And what are they?

Most people have a familiar handful of emotions they cycle through on repeat and wonder why nothing in their life changes. Want to do something different? Practice new emotions and see what behaviours follow.

By expanding your vocabulary of emotions, you can improve your range of feelings and instead of thinking you're scared, you may realise that you're just a little nervous, a bit perplexed, confused, or just plain irritated. Either way, you can choose to transmute the emotion and get on with your day.

Transmuting your emotions starts with awareness, and having a vocabulary of your range of emotions can help. I often share the Emotion Wheel with my clients as a simple tool to expand their vocabulary. A simple google search can find one.

When you're experiencing your emotions, you can run your eyes around the image of the wheel and determine what emotions you're feeling.

When you pinpoint what you're feeling on the wheel, you can stop and acknowledge what you're feeling. You may even be able to pinpoint what thought you had that activated that emotion and then reframe that thought. Otherwise, to transmute the feeling you ask yourself if what you are feeling is really how you want to feel about the situation. Is the feeling useful at that present moment?

And if not, you can instead, run your eyes again around the wheel and choose a more useful emotion. Once you've chosen which emotion you'd like to feel instead, close your eyes, remember a time when you felt that feeling and immerse yourself in that memory to generate that feeling in your body. It can be as simple as that. Then open your eyes and get on with your day.

If that doesn't work, then it's most likely because you're having a thought that is causing the negative emotion. Pinpoint what you were thinking before you felt the feeling and find a better feeling thought. Just like I did earlier when I found myself in the bathroom before my keynote, telling myself that I may be nervous, yes, but I could also be excited about stepping onto that stage. I replaced the meaning I had placed on the emotion, and it changed how I felt. That's how powerful the mind is.

So when Imposter Syndrome shows up as fear, ask yourself what emotion would be more useful in the current situation - would it be better to feel courageous, brave, curious, or excited? And then transmute the fear and take the next step toward your future.

Pretty powerful, hey?

So now we know we have the ability to transmute any emotion we feel, and that embracing a life of growth and expansion will require us to transmute fear when it shows up, we can then expect that fear will show up without feeling like we're a slave to that fear. This fear signal, however, is a sign of stepping outside your comfort zone. Let it happen, let it be OK.

If you want big things, you'll have to become the person that does big things.

Now it's time to become the next level version of yourself.

READY TO LEVEL UP YOUR IDENTITY?

Nine

UPDATE YOUR IDENTITY

"I STILL SOMETIMES FEEL LIKE A LOSER KID IN HIGH SCHOOL AND I JUST HAVE TO PICK MYSELF UP AND TELL MYSELF THAT I'M A SUPERSTAR EVERY MORNING SO THAT I CAN GET THROUGH THIS DAY AND BE FOR MY FANS WHAT THEY NEED FOR ME TO BE."

—*Lady Gaga*

About an hour or two into the Arizona event, I found myself sitting and listening to my mentors share how their lives had been so positively affected by being in rooms just like the one they were creating for us. They shared the conversations, opportunities, and expansion that had come from having the courage to join rooms like the one we were in. These rooms had created new partnerships, new business ideas, new client relationships, long-term connections, and referrals. Upon sharing this, my mentor also shared how uncomfortable it had been for her every time she put herself in those rooms. She shared how she felt like a fish out of water, an impostor, a fraud, and like she didn't belong.

She then turned to us and asked if anyone in the room felt like they didn't belong? As I raised my hand, I turned to look around the room. I was so surprised to see that almost everyone had their hands raised. My jaw dropped.

The host passed the microphone to someone in the back to share and as she started speaking, I recognised her. She had been a presenter for a group mastermind I was a part of years earlier. She had been an incredible speaker and I remember being so inspired by her that I had hit follow on Instagram, following along ever since.

Following her online I had learned about her journey of coming from nothing, not finishing school, and still building a million dollar business. She had grown a huge following and had been successful in business for so many years. But as we sat there in that room, she shared how she felt like she did not belong in a room with such successful people.

She spoke about how she felt like an impostor and she didn't believe she was good enough, qualified enough, educated enough, or successful enough to not only be in that room, but to contribute to the conversation. I could see the fear and shame on her face as she shared this.

I sat in utter shock. I could see deep down that this was her truth, and I couldn't believe it. This confident, outgoing, incredibly successful woman I'd come to know didn't believe she was good enough to be in *this* room. I found myself thinking, *Well if she's not good enough to be in this room, who is?? Definitely not me!*

Listening to her speak and share the reasons why she felt like she didn't belong, I could hear that she hadn't attributed her successes to who she was as a person today. It was as if she hadn't achieved anything. She couldn't acknowledge her own skills, wins, accomplishments, or accolades.

As she sat at the back of the room, speaking quietly into the microphone, it was as if she were five years old, a little girl who was so young, innocent and naive, and hadn't achieved anything in her life. But she had, she just couldn't acknowledge it.

This can happen when you don't stop to reflect and acknowledge your growth. Her identity — who she believed she was — hadn't caught up to everything she had achieved. She more than belonged in that room, heck, she had taught so many of us years earlier. She had shared valuable, experienced knowledge that I had personally applied to my business journey, yet here she was, riddled with Impostor Syndrome.

It was at this moment that I realised we don't ever *overcome* Imposter Syndrome, it will continue to show up in times of growth and expansion, when we put ourselves in rooms of successful people, yet if we don't learn to attribute our successes to who we are as people, and update our identity, we'll always feel like we don't belong.

At that moment, listening to this successful woman admit her insecurities, I wanted to run over and hug her and tell her that her brain was lying to her; that the story she was telling herself wasn't true, and it was time she updated her identity, because Imposter Syndrome is not something you have, it's not a disease you're diagnosed with where there's no cure. It's just protection. It's just thoughts.

Impostor Syndrome is something everyone experiences, but you can move through it and if you're savvy, you can learn to embrace it so it can become your superpower.

It was time for an identity upgrade so her brain could catch up with her current reality. Maybe it's time for you to have one as well. Use this powerful exercise to upgrade your identity.

Superpower Activation

#3: POWER OF REFLECTION & UPDATING YOUR IDENTITY

If you resonate with this story and realise that maybe it's time to update your identity, I want you to do this little activity.

Reflect on these questions:

- When you introduce yourself to others - how do you describe yourself?

- What past story is still playing on repeat in your head?

+ Which past version of yourself is running the show?

+ Which past experience of feeling unworthy is the old cassette tape stuck on repeat? Stopping you from seeing your real truth?

+ Where have you not update your identity? How are you still acting as an older version of you?

You are no longer that little girl or boy, you are so much more. And it's time to reflect and choose to update your biography, your story, your identity and attribute how far you've come to who you now are.

What is the real truth?

Write yourself a letter so your subconscious mind can be updated to your current reality.

Write down all of your accomplishments, achievements, awards, accolades, education, what you've overcome, and what you're capable of up until this day. Don't stop writing until you've written for at least 10 minutes straight.

Start the sentence off with:
It's now (insert current year) *I'm no longer that little child anymore and I am capable of . . .*

UPDATE YOUR IDENTITY

Throughout the book there are multiple Superpower Activations and Resources - Head to www.christinecorcoran.com.au/impostor-book for all the resources mentioned.

WHEN NEW REFERENCE POINTS ARE ACKNOWLEDGED YOU UPGRADE YOUR IDENTITY

Fast forward four months and once again I was flying to Los Angeles for event #2 in Beverly Hills. This time, I knew what to expect. I now knew some of the people attending and I was looking forward to a magical few days. I had even booked to stay at the luxurious hotel where the event was hosted. Boasting five star luxury and situated one block from Rodeo Drive, it was truly star studded. As I drove in, the entrance was surrounded with luxury cars and security (talk about an identity upgrade). I also booked a photoshoot to do the day after the event because, why not? I wanted to capture this experience.

The day of the event, I caught up with some connections for coffee and to create some content before heading to the conference room. I walked in, grabbed my name tag, and started meeting and chatting with new people.

I reconnected with familiar faces and continued our conversations as the doors opened and we headed in to find seats. The way I walked into that room was in complete contrast with the first event I had attend four months prior. I wasn't nervous, I was excited. I wasn't apprehensive, I was prepared. Yes, some of that confidence did come from the past reference point of knowing what to expect; I knew I wouldn't be walking into a room of strangers. But it also came from feeling like I belonged. My identity had been upgraded.

I now knew that I was the type of person who flew halfway across the world to attend events like this. I was the type of person who connected with other incredible entrepreneurs and added value. I was accomplished and knowledgeable and I belonged in this room as much as anybody else did.

Did my Impostor Syndrome show up? Absolutely. Did I let it stop me? Certainly not.

This time I got so much more involved. I raised my hand, and spoke to the guest speakers. I asked *big* questions. I put my hat in the ring and asked to be considered for new opportunities, and I gave advice that was valuable and well received by people more successful than me.

At the event, I distinctly remember three interactions that levelled up my identity. The first one occurred when I was speaking to someone who I have looked up to for years. We were having a conversation and she was sharing about a problem she was having with a new offering she had launched. In a couple of questions we uncovered what the problem was and I gave her specific steps to take to rectify it. I could see the clarity this conversation gave her and she was very grateful.

The second, was a conversation with a marketing agency owner and he was sharing a challenge they were having with increasing sales for an offer they had previously launched. After listening and asking a few questions, I also gave him some advice as to what I felt was right, and he turned around and said, "That was the most valuable piece of advice I've gotten all day."

In these moments the thought, *See I do belong here and I do have value to add,* rang in my mind, attributing the experience to who I am.

The third was scary and I am so proud of myself with how I handled it. It was at the end of the night, and one of my friends was trying to muster the courage to speak to the host of the event about possibly investing in her NFP, and she was stalling. I coached her into approaching him and supported her in going along to ensure she made the ask. After speaking with her, he turned to me and thanked me for flying so far to be there and asked how he could support *me*. I was not expecting this. I was taken aback, because he had already helped me so much so far, but I couldn't let this opportunity pass me by. I already had a prepared ask in preparation for the event, so I was ready.

I asked him to connect me with other high-level entrepreneurs that run events, groups, and masterminds, and to recommend me as a speaker. I shared the unique topics I could present on and asked if it was OK if I emailed him the details to make it easy for him to share my name. He was so gracious and already thought of a few people he could approach and vowed to make the connections. I was blown away.

Mountains move when you're willing to embrace Imposter Syndrome, transmute the fear, and move forward.

I would never have had the courage to do this if it wasn't for the work I had done to anticipate Impostor Syndrome, transmute the fear, and embrace every opportunity. This wouldn't have been possible months earlier. I would have crumbled and probably said, "No there's nothing I need help with," and ran away and hid. Instead I stood tall, spoke with confidence, and went for it.

And you can too.

It's time to learn how to embrace Imposter Syndrome so you can dance with it as you take the scary action and achieve big things.

It's time for step 2: Embrace it.

STEP TWO

Embrace It

Ten

WELCOME THE FEAR

Before starting my business, I was in a sales role for 6+ years for a global luxury goods company. As part of my role, we were expected to walk into new businesses, approach complete strangers, introduce ourselves, and ask them to buy from us.

The awkward responses and rejection were intense. Our KPI's were to walk into 6-8 new businesses a day, and get rejected (sign new business actually, but you get the idea). There were days I would sit in my car out front or down the street from the business I was supposed to walk into, pumping myself up, convincing myself to get out of the car, rip the bandaid off, and just do it. Some days it worked, others it didn't.

After years and years of doing this, I developed a thick skin for rejection, even though it never got "easier". I just got braver and learned to develop better strategies.

Instead of fearing the rejection, I welcomed it. Instead of getting anxious of what they were going to say, and how they were going to kick me out of their business, I created new ways to have interesting conversations, and learned never to run from the rejection. I would play games with colleagues with how many times we could get rejected that day, or how long we could have a conversation with someone before telling them what company we were from.

The trick was to never run from the rejection, as more conversations led to more conversions. Plus, I learned to never let the fear thoughts get too out of control before stepping through the front door.

My brain can run rampant with all the end of the world scenarios, picturing people chasing me out the door, yelling at me, or calling the police. Haha. None of these ever eventuated. Yes, there were plenty of unwelcome conversations, but none that ever got abusive or dramatic. I would always remind myself just before opening the door that to them, I could be a potential customer, so they have to be nice to me. Their role was customer service. They'll be nice. Then I would step in, smile, and approach whoever I was on a mission to talk to.

Instead of letting my brain go to the worse case scenarios, I learned to train my brain to support me rather than derail me. I would sit in my car, pump myself up, mentally rehearsing scenarios in my head of the interaction going well, telling myself that maybe they're waiting for me to arrive, maybe they'd be excited to chat with me. I would imagine the scenario ending with a positive outcome. Whenever I did this, I always felt more positive stepping in the door. My internal positivity would garner a more positive response instead of walking in with fear on my face, waiting for the rejection.

I never realised how much these experiences prepared me for running my own business until I had to start promoting myself online. These scenarios built resilience. When challenged by hard or daunting things in my new business, I could look back fondly on those years and remind myself that at least I didn't have to do *that* ever again.

Learning to not run from the rejection became such a resilient behaviour that also taught me to not respond to the fear of Impostor Syndrome. When doing scary things that could lead to rejection, judgement, failure or humiliation, you have to expect that a little fear is going to show up. Just like you would embrace a loyal long-term friend, you must embrace the fear/Impostor Syndrome and appreciate it for protecting you. Ultimately, it's just warning you of the possible danger. When you know Impostor Syndrome is going to be present, and you learn to embrace it instead of running from it, you can do great things. When you accept that it's just a pause along the path, not the end of the road, you learn to keep moving toward Impostor Syndrome, and not shy away from the fear.

The more aware you become, the easier it is to work with. Your brain knows exactly what arsenal of thoughts to use against you, it knows exactly what to say that will cause you to freeze in fear and stop you in your tracks. The beauty of your brain is that it's lazy. It will use the same saying over and over again, and if you take the power out of those words and flip the script, you'll get to take back control and choose how you want to proceed. And the interesting thing is, the sayings or thoughts, are the same for a lot of people:

Who am I?

I'm not good enough/experienced enough/qualified enough. I'm not ___enough for ___.

WELCOME THE FEAR

Who do I think I am? I'm not an expert. They're going to figure out I'm a fraud.

It's universal. No matter who I talk to, what country they're from, their walk of life, or upbringing, the fear thoughts are the same. Sometimes there are small nuances, but generally they're the same. What is the common saying Impostor Syndrome uses for you? The more aware of the specific words it repeats when the fear arises, the easier it is for you to embrace and flip.

Superpower Activation

#4: HOW DOES IMPOSTOR SYNDROME SHOW UP FOR YOU?

Take a few minutes to journal on this question to truly uncover how the Impostor Syndrome shows up for you.

What does your Impostor Syndrome say to you when you're trying to uplevel?

Most people don't realise they have the power to change their own thoughts and so they believe what their brain is telling them. These thoughts, though, aren't entirely true and if you signed up to live a big life, you're going to have to master changing your thoughts to be more useful ones that support the action you want to take and the results you're eager to achieve. Otherwise you'll never get out of your own way.

If you don't, those thoughts will hold power over you and derail your dreams.

Now that you're aware of your thoughts, the next step in turning the impostor into your superpower is learning to flip the script.

Throughout the book there are multiple Superpower Activations and Resources - Head to www.christinecorcoran.com.au/impostor-book for all the resources mentioned.

Twelve

FLIP THE SCRIPT

"THE GREATEST OBSTACLE FOR ME HAS BEEN THE VOICE IN MY HEAD THAT I CALL MY OBNOXIOUS ROOMMATE. I WISH SOMEONE WOULD INVENT A TAPE RECORDER THAT WE COULD ATTACH TO OUR BRAINS TO RECORD EVERYTHING WE TELL OURSELVES. WE WOULD REALIZE HOW IMPORTANT IT IS TO STOP THIS NEGATIVE SELF-TALK. IT MEANS PUSHING BACK AGAINST OUR OBNOXIOUS ROOMMATE WITH A DOSE OF WISDOM."

—*Arianna Huffington*, FOUNDER AND CEO OF THRIVE GLOBAL AND FOUNDER OF HUFFINGTON POST.

Most people have about 60-70,000 thoughts a day and 90% of them are repetitive thoughts from yesterday, according to a study by Fred Luskin of Stanford University. Our brains are a well oiled machine that loves to follow patterns of thought to preserve energy so repeated safe patterns of thought is one way it does this.

But don't take your thoughts as gospel. In fact, it's time to question every single one of them. Thoughts are repetitive patterns that have a certain outcome. Your brain continues to repeat them for certainty and safety, but what if they aren't even true? And more importantly, if they're not cheering you on, guiding you to take the step towards greatness, why do you listen to them? If a friend of yours belittled you, judged you and told you that you weren't good enough to achieve your goals, would you listen to them? Would you stay friends with them? I'd hope not.

> **BELIEFS ARE JUST THOUGHTS YOU'VE HAD MANY TIMES, IT DOES NOT MEAN THEY'RE ALWAYS TRUE.**

When we have a friend or someone we love who doubts themselves, aren't we the first ones to lift them up and disagree with the doubtful words they've just uttered? We think, *'they're so talented, capable, and worthy, they're deserving of anything they want.'*

It's so interesting how we can see the goodness and talent in others, but when it comes to ourselves, we doubt our worthiness. All we can see are our flaws, inexperience, lack of talent, and not enough-ness.

Let me ask you this…

If your Impostor Syndrome thoughts are causing you to get stuck in fear and are preventing you from living up to your fullest potential, are they serving you?

Remember, just because you thought something, does not mean it's true.

As you've probably gathered already, you mindset (thoughts) are pretty influential. They impact how you feel. Your feelings then drive your behaviour and your behaviour (actions) create your results. So to change the results, you must first change your thoughts.

It's time to flip the script on those thoughts and learn to use your thoughts to encourage courageous action.

The best way to flip the script on Impostor Syndrome is to do two things:

1. Question the fuck out of it, because often the thoughts have no proof, or are a gross misrepresentation of reality and,

2. Reframe the thought and change it to something more useful.

Identify which one was your most common thought and work through that section below:

Let's start with:

WHO AM I?

So who are you? Why do you want to do that big scary thing? Why is it important to you?

And in the words of Turia Pitt, Who are you not to? If you're capable, then you must. You may not have the experience yet but how are you going to get it if you don't do the damn thing?

You will never know what you're capable of until you give it a try. When you have the thought, *Who am I? What is it in reference to?* Are you comparing yourself to other people? Are you worrying about someone's judgment? Maybe you're worried about being judged on your accomplishments, past, or experiences? Lack of knowledge? (we explore this further with "*I am not an expert*" below.)

Is it time you upgraded your identity, as we spoke about earlier? Could you add value in this space? Could you inspire others?

If it's on your heart to do it, then why not you?

Even if there are more qualified, experienced, or better people out there who could, who cares? If it's something you want to do, then you must do it. Not just to see if you can, but to prove to yourself that you're capable. Nothing else needs to matter. Even if it's already been done or already exists, if it's on your heart, you must.

You'll bring your own unique flavour to it.

Plus, maybe the person who will benefit from you creating it or speaking on it, needs you to share it in order for them to receive it.

Don't underestimate the impact you could have. There have been some amazing creations that, God forbid, if they had been tossed aside on the first try, or the creator had listened to the Impostor Syndrome, they wouldn't exist. If Mark Zuckerberg had thought 'Well, Myspace exists, who am I to think I can create anything better." Facebook wouldn't exist!!

If it's in reference to fear of judgment, then ask yourself, who are you fearing the judgment of most? Who specifically? Why them? What are you worried about them saying? Does their opinion really matter to you? Are they an important person in your life? Maybe you need to ask them for support?

Instead of fearing their judgement, ask for support; you'd be surprised in the response you'll get. Anytime this comes up for me, I remind myself that when someone judges, or gives an opinion on something you're doing, but they're not in the arena taking scary action, putting themselves out there, then they're probably just speaking from their own fears and doubts.

If you don't do something just because you're fearing the judgment, how will that make you feel in the long run?

Really think about this.

Will you be disappointed in yourself? You have to ask yourself these questions because if you're living in fear of others' judgement, then you're not really living. Yes others judge, but their judgement shouldn't matter more than your opinion of yourself and you living your fullest life. I'd rather be judged by others, than be disappointed in myself for not trying. I don't want to regret not living the life I want to live.

Flip the script on 'WHO AM I?' And replace it with, 'WHO AM I NOT TO?'

When you ask better questions, you'll not only get better answers, but they'll motivate you to take better action.

WHO DO YOU THINK YOU ARE?

This Impostor Syndrome thought used to play in my mind all the time like a broken record or a Spice Girl Song; try not to sing that over and over. Especially when I started hosting events in Brisbane back in 2018. I initially started them because I wanted to be a speaker and knew I needed to grow my community. I even roped in one of my best friends to co-host with me because I didn't feel anywhere near confident enough to run an event on my own. What if I didn't know what to say? What if I couldn't answer the questions from the crowd? What if everyone laughed at me and never returned? All the Impostor Syndrome thoughts ran through my mind.

My friend and co-host designed a pretty graphic to promote the first event. The flyer had our two faces on it with our names and titles, and I remember thinking, *who do we think we are?* People aren't going to attend, we're nobodies. We're not the big, flashy names people usually choose to listen to. This idea had to be insane.

Yet we had 22 people show up to our first event, lots of friends and family members, but also strangers we'd never met before, to be sure. As everyone was arriving in the little space we had hired, the room was loud with all the women chatting. I remember looking at my friend/co-host with my stomach in my throat, knowing it was time to start. She looked back at me with a flushed face and utter fear in her eyes and I knew I had to step up and not show any fear so we wouldn't both make a dash for the exit.

We welcomed everyone to take a seat and miraculously everything flowed smoothly. My co-host and I bounced off each other seamlessly, getting the audience involved, sharing their experiences, and creating opportunities for the women in the room to chat and connect. At one point we'd given a direction to chat amongst themselves with a specific topic and the room was a buzz with positive energy. I had a moment to pull my co-host to the side and reflect on how things were going, we were more than half way through the event, there was no turning back now.

There were moments when everyone was looking to us to speak where I had to calm my nerves and focus on what I was there to share, but the overwhelming lesson that came through that night was that we are all the same. When asking women in the room to share their thoughts and experiences, they too were fearful of being judged. When I focused on sharing my experience, there was no fear of judgement. I wasn't trying to be the expert or the know-it-all, I was there to create a connection and share my story.

We continued to run events each month, growing and expanding them. My co-host decided to step away after the fourth event to focus on other endeavours, but I felt a responsibility to the community we had been building, and so I continued to run them almost monthly for three years straight. It was challenging yet rewarding and I got to connect with some amazing leaders and business people over the years, making new friends and getting to learn from some incredible guest speakers.

Every month people continued to show up and bring their friends. Even now, people remember the events fondly and ask me to run them again.

This never would have happened if I listened to that little voice in my head say, *who do you think you are?*

Let's flip the script from 'who do you think you are,' and instead replace it with something like: 'I have value to add to the world.'

AM I GOOD ENOUGH?

This Impostor Syndrome thought is super common. The Impostor loves to use some form of this question, *Am I good enough to do this? Am I good enough to ask for this? Go after that? Am I experienced enough? Qualified enough? Talented enough? Worthy enough?*

When questioning this thought, ask yourself: *What is enough? What do you mean by enough?* For you to do this thing (whatever it is) how enough do you have to be?

The term 'enough' has no measurement. It has no boundaries, and this makes it an intangible goal or an impossible achievement. Does someone ever feel 'enough'?

Then consider this: what if we were actually asking the wrong question?

I always love to come back to the explanation that, "you only need to be two steps ahead of those you want to help." With this in mind, ask yourself, *do I know enough to help those I want to help? Do I know enough for me to start taking action on the thing I want to do? Am I qualified enough, smart enough, experienced enough to contribute value here?*

Whenever I have a client come up against this story, of not feeling enough, it often comes back to a time in their childhood when they didn't feel 'good enough'. Once I have helped them heal this part of their past, they can learn to see themselves as who they are now, not the child they once were, who at that time wasn't experienced enough, qualified enough, or old enough to know better, or do better. Now as an adult, they have a lot to offer the world.

It also comes back to questioning your capabilities and the fear of the unknown. If you haven't been taught to acknowledge your growth and achievements along the way, then the brain most likely hasn't developed strong enough reference points for you to feel like you are enough.

You are enough, you just haven't acknowledged that yet. (More on how to rewire your brain for this soon.)

This question could also be underpinned with the thought, *am I deserving? Am I enough to receive this? Am I (deserving) enough to have this opportunity?*

The answer is always yes. Your worth is not determined by anyone else. It is not determined by your achievements, your education, or your successes. You are enough. Full stop. Existing on this planet, being born at this point in time, being in this situation, means you are enough. You were born deserving. There is no one more or less deserving on this planet. It's time you started to believe this.

Your worth, your deservedness, is not up for debate or measurement. There is no question about it, so stop letting your brain take you there. If an opportunity is being offered to you, if it's on your heart to go after it, then you're deserving of it. In fact, I'll go as far to say it's on your path because it's preparing you for something greater in the future. So let this be the moment you decide that you're worthy of it all.

You're enough. You're deserving. You just have to believe it.

So let's flip the script and turn this one on its head.

Rather than letting your mind demand of you, *am I enough?* Learn to ask, *can I contribute here? Yes, then I will.*

I'M NOT AN EXPERT

Oh the Impostor Syndrome OG. I'm sure we've all thought this and will again. And boy does it pack a punch.

What even is an expert? If you look it up in the Collins English Dictionary the definition of an expert is as follows:

EXPERT; NOUN;
A PERSON WHO IS VERY KNOWLEDGEABLE ABOUT OR SKILFUL IN A PARTICULAR AREA.

Who deems someone to be an expert? How knowledgeable do you have to be? I've often heard that an expert is someone who's done 10,000 hours of work on a topic, which could be true, but I've also seen people online name themselves an expert without any proof or foundation. Which one is correct? I sometimes feel this can muddy the waters of truth and causes us to not know who to believe.

I have even been called a mindset expert, expert on Impostor Syndrome, and sales expert by others who have seen my work or heard me speak. Does it mean that it's true? You tell me. Am I knowledgeable? Yes. Do I have 10,000 hours of work under my belt, yes. But that person doesn't know that for sure. I'm not even sure if they would know my qualifications, and yet, they call me an expert.

I wonder if it's just because people like to know how to place others. It's easy to think someone's an expert when we see them speak confidently on a topic and deem them to be knowledgeable.

So if your brain is saying "I am not an expert," it could be true, or it might not be. I've seen so many incredibly talented and highly educated people get caught in the trap of Impostor Syndrome, with this statement running through their mind. Yet when we explore their skills, talents, and education, they're more educated than a lot of people out there in the same space being called experts.

I see clients get caught in self sabotaging behaviours like the trap of over consuming and going after the next qualification, degree, PhD, never feeling like they know enough. And let's be honest, the more you learn, it can feel like the less you know.

So I bring this back to the statement I made earlier: can you contribute? Can you add value? Can you help those who are two steps behind?

Be mindful who you're thinking of when you're worried about not being an expert on a particular subject. Rather than worrying about being seen as the expert in the eyes of your past professors, past colleagues, or bosses, refocus your attention on the people you want to serve.

Can you help them? Do you know more than them? Yes? Then it's up to you to share it. You don't have to be *the* expert, but you can still contribute and add value.

Which brings me to my next question: how does one even become an expert?

In my opinion, it's not just learning and gaining more knowledge, it's putting that knowledge to use. Either teaching someone or speaking on the topic until you have the ability to make it more succinct and you become known as the go-to person on that topic. Maybe the official definition is 10,000 hours of practice, but you have to remember that you have to do the thing to get the 10,000 hours of experience. It's OK to be in the process of becoming, and still share your journey and knowledge along the way. You don't need to wait until the benchmark of 10,000 hours to begin helping people. Even doctors practice on real people before they're fully qualified, I'm sure you can practice your skill and put yourself out there.

Becoming an expert on a topic doesn't come from sitting behind a book or a laptop learning more, unless you know zero about the subject you want to speak on.

You could spend 90 days speaking on a specific topic that you'd like to be seen as an expert on, and very quickly your audience would start seeing you as that expert. You could give a Ted Talk, write a book, produce some videos, and be seen as an expert on that one subject. And to do all or any of those things, you're going to have to navigate through the fear to take the action.

We must remember that the experts you see out in the world sharing their knowledge and expertise, they weren't recognised as experts when they first began to share their wisdom. It's often after they've been sharing consistently for some time that they get labeled a true expert on the topic.

Take Brene Brown for instance; she is now a world renowned expert on shame and vulnerability but she gave talks about vulnerability for several years before her Tedx

Talk in 2010 that became one of the most viewed TEDx talks of all time, "The Power of Vulnerability".

Do you have the courage to move through the fear, reframe this thought, and start sharing your expertise?

Alex Hermozi spoke about this when he launched his recent book, *$100M Leads,* where he spoke about the fact that you can be as prepared as possible and still experience anxiety and fear-based thoughts. He practiced his webinar to publicly launch his book to hundreds of thousands of people three times a day, every day, for months until he had memorised it. On his **podcast**, Alex spoke about having anxiety leading up to the launch. He coped by practicing his webinar even more, saying, "you're right to have anxiety, If you don't have anxiety you probably haven't practiced it enough." He realised it was part of the process. Not something that you bypass.

So instead of thinking you have to be an expert to start, flip the script and say to yourself instead:

I'm willing to contribute. I'm in the process of becoming and sharing my wisdom and expertise is part of that process. I have the courage to start where I am and develop the expertise.

It's also key to be mindful to not get stuck in comparison to other experts and discount what you can contribute and what you bring to the table.

You're unique as you are and that's worth acknowledging.

Ask yourself, *in relation to what I want to do—WHAT DO I BRING TO THE TABLE? How can I contribute and add value here?*

Make a list of everything that you bring to the table. What conjures up this Impostor Syndrome thought telling you that you're not an expert?

Another way to ask this wound be, Why are *you* the best person to do this thing?

Spend at least ten minutes writing down all the reasons why you're the best person to do this thing and everything that you'll bring to it, just like I did with the podcast.

Before you know it, you'll have a list of reasons why you are the best person to help the people you want to help or speak on the topic you want to speak on. You're more knowledgeable on your expertise than you give yourself credit for and it's got nothing to do with whether you know *everything* on the topic, because that's physically impossible. There is no one person that knows absolutely everything on any topic. They may know a lot, yes, but it's impossible to be sure that they know everything.

So stop listening to that Imposter Syndrome thought and remind yourself what you have to offer. You're more than qualified to get started and start helping those who need you.

THEY'RE GOING TO FIGURE OUT I'M A FRAUD!

"I HAVE WRITTEN 11 BOOKS, BUT EACH TIME I THINK, 'UH OH, THEY'RE GOING TO FIND OUT NOW. I'VE RUN A GAME ON EVERYBODY, AND THEY'RE GOING TO FIND ME OUT.'"

—Maya Angelou

Who are you fooling? They're going to see right through you, they're going to see you're a full blown fraud. Ever thought this before? I have, I'm sure you have. This thought is also common. This often comes up even when you've got evidence from the past that you're capable, or even that you're worthy of the thing you're about to do, but still your brain warns you to stay in a lane of comfort.

This little statement is a warning of possible danger from our evolved human brain. Our brains are always trying to protect us from danger and the fear of being ostracised from our tribe is one that comes from caveman days where being ostracised from your tribe would mean certain death. This evolutionary fear is still one that shows up to protect us even though that kind of danger isn't as much of a reality for modern humans. Unlike cavemen days, we may no longer die if we're excluded from our family or circle of friends, but the fear persists.

Even so, we still want to be accepted and kept safe within our family unit or friends groups.

This becomes dangerous, however, when people don't attribute their skills, growth, or knowledge to where they currently are in life, and are outsourcing their sense of worthiness to other people. The dependence, rather than acting as protection, can become debilitating. Just like in the Maya Angelou quote above, she was worried other people wouldn't deem her acceptable. She doubted whether she really did have the skill or knowledge for people to not call her a fraud.

Even with eleven books under her belt, many of which are award winning novels, she still doubted her skills and abilities because she most likely hadn't updated her identity and attributed her accomplishments, knowledge, and achievements to who she was at the present time. She must first accept herself and believe in the value she brings to the world rather than looking to others to validate her.

There are ways to flip the script and take your power back when this Impostor Syndrome arsenal shows up. There are two parts to flipping the script on this internal Impostor Syndrome thought.

PART ONE - ATTRIBUTING YOUR PAST ACCOMPLISHMENTS, ACHIEVEMENTS, AND SKILLS TO WHO YOU ARE TODAY.

So often we move from one project to the next, never stopping to actually acknowledge what we've done or how we've grown. If we don't attribute the accomplishments, achievements, and skills we've developed to our identity, our minds still think we're the person we were a year ago. This past version of ourselves doesn't have all those new capabilities. When we don't upgrade our beliefs about ourselves (our identity), we can get stuck in this fear based myth of others not believing our expertise or deservedness. In a later chapter I'll explore more about how to get unstuck from this as we learn to celebrate our wins.

PART TWO - USE FREEDOM STATEMENTS.

I learned this from Lori Harder, hearing her speak on stages and reading her book, *A Tribe Called Bliss*. If you're stuck with Impostor Syndrome, worrying about getting it wrong, being seen as a fraud, or being judged for not knowing what you're talking about, learn to use freedom statements before sharing your thoughts or opinion.

A freedom statement allows you to share your thoughts on a topic, without positioning yourself as an expert.

Try these before sharing your opinion:
I'm new to this, so forgive me, here's how I think about this:
I'm not an expert on this topic, I can only speak from my experience.
This is just my perspective, and I might be wrong, but here's what I'm thinking...
I could be off here, but what if we consider...
I'm not sure if this is the right approach, but what about...
This is just one possibility, so feel free to disagree, but what if we...
I haven't fully thought this through yet, but one idea could be...
I'm still figuring this out, but maybe we could..
I might be missing something, but my initial thought is...

This is just a thought, and I'm open to other ideas, but how about...
I could be wrong, but I wonder if...

Try one of these next time you're sharing something you don't feel you're an expert in or fully confident in, and see how it lets you off the fear-hook and allows you to feel more confident in sharing your opinion/message.

WHAT IF I GET IT WRONG?

"What if I get it wrong" is another common Impostor Syndrome thought, and to be honest, there is always a risk of getting something wrong, but this doesn't mean you shouldn't do something.

With growth comes risk. There is always a risk of something not working out, of someone judging you. Ideas fail. But a life without risk is a life not lived. You'll regret not taking the risk, more than getting it wrong. You have to be willing to take a little risk because the payoff is always worth more than the regret you'll feel for not trying the thing.

The best way to flip this thought, is to ask yourself - *WHAT IF I GET IT RIGHT? What if it works out better than I ever imagined?*

This reminds me of that poem by Erin Hanson:

> THERE IS FREEDOM WAITING FOR YOU,
> ON THE BREEZES OF THE SKY,
> AND YOU ASK, "WHAT IF I FALL?"
> OH, BUT MY DARLING,
> WHAT IF YOU FLY?

Our brains are wired with a negative bias as a way to keep us safe. We must train our brains to focus on the positive. If you train your brain to look at the positive and ask better questions, you'll get better answers. If we ask ourselves, *what if I get it wrong?* Our brain will probably answer, "That would be bad, so you better not do it." And probably conjure up end of the world scenarios keeping you in fear.

Remember, your brain is always looking for danger, and when there is a risk, it wants you to stay on the safest side of that risk. Most of the time that means not to do the new or risky thing you're considering. But not doing it isn't going to get you to where you want to be.

If you constantly avoid risk, will you create the life you want to live?

When you're focused on what could go wrong, the last thing you'll want to do is take action. But if we ask, "what if it works out, what if it goes right," we're more likely to follow through. So choose a more empowering thought and you'll always be the person who goes after what they want.

So flip the script from "What if I get it wrong" to "What if I get it right?" and go after your dreams with fearless abandon.

Want more mindset flips?
Head to www.christinecorcoran.com.au/impostor-book

Thirteen

BUILD A BANK OF EVIDENCE

One of my favourite tools to share with clients to help them overcome that pesky Impostor Syndrome and strengthen their self belief is building a bank of evidence. Anytime I'm creating something new or doing something I've never done before, and that old story of not feeling good enough pops into my head, I build a bank of evidence to bolster my self belief and to support the action I want to take.

It's quite easy to forget all the incredible things you've achieved and all the things that you've learned along your journey because your brain pushes that to the side to focus on what's important in the moment. When you're about to do something new, your brain focuses on the uncertainty or danger, all the worst case scenarios to keep you safe. It's at this moment that you need to redirect your attention to the evidence you have from the past that will set you up to succeed and be courageous despite the fear of trying something new.

When I started my podcast, my events, and began pitching for speaking gigs, I built a bank of evidence every time. Now, I keep it on my desktop so it's easy to find when I need a little reminder of all the courageous things I've done.

Start with thinking of something in the near future you'd like to do that may activate Impostor Syndrome.

Sit for 10 minutes and write down all the reasons why you're the best person to do that thing. At first your brain will throw at you, *you're not the best person to do this, I'm sure there's plenty of better people to do this.*

Which may be true, but it doesn't matter. Push all of those thoughts to the side and keep asking yourself, *What makes me the best person to do this?*

Superpower Activation

#5: CREATE YOUR BANK OF EVIDENCE

Gather all the evidence from the past to prove to yourself (and your brain) that you're capable of doing the thing you've set out to do. Know that you are the best person for this.

Answer this questions and write it all down.

What makes me the best person to do this? What do I bring to the table?

Think back to all the experiences, education, and knowledge you've searched for and mastered. All the times you've overcome something, achieved something, and if it will make you the best candidate to do that thing, get it all down on paper. Keep writing for a full ten minutes. Usually some of the best proof you'll find is after you take time to reflect on the years of your life and explore the depths of your mind. If you haven't stepped back to explore your past, it will be difficult to understand the skills and experiences that will help you today.

Write down each decade of your life and reflect on the skills, abilities, experiences, education, accomplishments, and lessons you have learned throughout the years that could support you with what you want to do next. It may feel challenging to think back to your earlier years, but the longer you sit and focus on it the more memories will flow.

0-10
10-20
20-30
40-50 and so on.

Don't stop until you've got a big list. If you keep asking the question, *what part of my life experience will support me here and now? What makes me the best person to do this?* You will always find an answer. Your brain will sift through experiences to find more and more evidence that makes you the best person to do the specific thing you seek to do. Trust me, you'll be so surprised with what your subconscious mind will remember.

Throughout the book there are multiple Superpower Activations and Resources - Head to **www.christinecorcoran.com.au/impostor-book** for all the resources mentioned.

BUILD A BANK OF EVIDENCE

I did this for myself when I launched my podcast. I had all the reasons to not do it: I was early on in my business, inexperienced in podcasting, and was nobody anyone would elect to listen to. But it was something I wanted to do. I sat for ten minutes and wrote down all the reasons why I was the best person to launch that specific podcast.

Remember the reasons from earlier in the book:

The reason you want to start one is a legitimate reason – you want to help people and that's worthy of following through on even if it doesn't work out.

You're educated on the topic and you know how to break things down so it's simple and practical for people to learn from. Besides, this shit could change someone's life. It could change mine!

You have lots of experiences to share that people will find value from, your stories could help someone change their lives.

You've studied, educated yourself, and applied yourself in ways that are unique to your experience and this would be so valuable to others to hear. This life-changing wisdom needs to be shared.

You don't have to call yourself an expert, you can just share from your experience.

I kept digging into my past and reflecting on all the things I'd learned and achieved. Doing this activation I remembered a time in high school when I took an elective on how to be a radio presenter. I don't remember why I signed up for it, I never used those skills for anything until I began my podcast. How bizarre, I thought, that those lessons would come to help create a podcast.

This last golden nugget of evidence only presented itself after reflecting on my past for ten whole minutes. A memory I had completely forgotten until this exercise.

The more you explore your mind the more evidence you'll find. Your brain is so focused on protecting you that unless you ask the right questions, you'll only get the fear-based response.

This evidence will bolster confidence in yourself and then when you apply it to the thing you're about to do, it will give you proof that you'll be able to figure it out and the fear will start to dissipate.

There are two things you're looking for as you step into the unknown and embrace a new challenge:

- Proof that you've done something slightly similar so your brain switches off the fight or flight response. Similarity breeds familiarity and that brings an element of certainty and safety to this new thing you're about to do. Finding nuggets of proof reduces the fear response.

- Reasons why *you* should absolutely do the thing. These reasons, as outlined above, can range from your lived experience, to training, to past career endeavours.

Once you have your list, take a moment to reflect over the list and notice how you feel. Do you feel less afraid? Do you feel slightly more confident and capable in moving toward taking action? Hopefully yes, and once you do, you can move onto doing bigger and harder things.

GET SOCIAL PROOF AND FEEDBACK FROM YOUR CUSTOMERS TO GET MORE EVIDENCE

Another way to gain more evidence to bolster your self belief is to ensure you document it from past clients and businesses you've worked with (even past bosses and colleagues you worked with). Oftentimes we create great results and outcomes for clients, or help them to achieve great things, but forget to ask the right questions to get the appropriate feedback.

There have been countless times where I've explored this with clients of my own where I've asked for a testimonial but left it completely up to them to reflect and report back. When the testimonial finally came back, it was surface level and basic.

It's great when clients say nice things, yes, but it doesn't really get to the evidence we need to believe that we're good at what we do and having a positive impact on our clients. Before asking for a testimonial, make sure you do a review yourself of the progress the client has made, the wins they or the business had along the way, and review any data to pull the facts. Be sure to also ask them to do the same, otherwise they may not even look at the data. Then, when asking for a testimonial, ask specific questions to elicit a better response. Such as:

- What has (insert specific result/outcome) done for you and your business?

- What was your favourite part of working together?

- What has changed since we started working together?

- What specific results has our work had an impact on?

- If you hadn't worked with us, what may not have happened?

- What tangible results have you noticed that relate to our work together?

- What impact has this had on your bottom line? What impact has this had on your self confidence? What impact has it had on your ability to attract or convert more clients? What other benefits have you noticed?

Ask better questions, and you'll get better answers. If you don't ask the right questions you may never know the impact your work has had for that client.

I have a folder on my laptop of all the kind things clients have said to me. It's filled with testimonials, messages, social media tags, and feedback from survey forms. Anytime I'm doubting my worth or impact, I read over them to remind myself of how powerful my work is.

Anytime some positive feedback comes in, I take a moment to truly appreciate it. I don't "need" it, but sometimes a little reminder of how badass you are feels good. Keep a record of your testimonials so when you need to build out your bank of evidence for something new you're about to do, you'll have heaps to pull from.

What if there is no evidence?

Sometimes, when I'm stepping into the unknown and doing something not remotely familiar, I sit down to write my bank of evidence. I ask my brain, *what have I done in the past that has prepared me for this*? If I'm doing something new, my brain comes up blank.

So I ask, *what's something similar?* And again, my brain comes up with nothing. Sometimes I have to sit there longer until I find something. Racking my brain, looking for something similar. After some time, my brain will come up with a few things, but it does not dissipate my fear. I remind myself that just because I haven't done something like this before, does not mean that I cannot do it.

There are plenty of things that I've done without prior experience. There have been times where I've done something so completely new, and of course I survived.

When I was 21 I left Australia indefinitely and traveled to the other side of the world to join and work on a cruise ship. In the process of joining, I had to fly from my small country town in Gippsland, Victoria, Australia to Santiago, Chile, and then take an hour long taxi to Valparaiso where I was to meet the ship. I didn't speak the language, I had never flown on a plane alone before, and I remember standing on that dock, looking up at this ginormous cruise liner as big as a skyscraper and thinking to myself, *I can't believe I got here alone, and am about to live on this huge ship for the next eight months?* I was so far from home, not knowing what to expect, and not knowing anyone.

Was I fearless doing this? No. Was I brave? Hell yes. Did I die? No. So I know I can do things I've never done before.

WHEN THE EVIDENCE ISN'T THERE, YOU'VE GOT TO CREATE IT.

Confidence only comes after you take the step and do the action. You're never confident before the action as much as people would have you believe. If you don't have evidence that you can do something, you have to go out and create that evidence. The more you overcome your fear time and time again, the more proof you'll have for your brain to know that you can not only do hard things, but that you're someone that doesn't let fear win.

Finding something similar to what you seek to do makes your brain feel even 10% safer. You can transfer the confidence from one thing into another by finding similarities. You can even borrow confidence from other people or other areas of your life; just act confident until you've taken the action. Even when I'm faced with new, scary things, I think back to times from my past where I took big scary actions and remember how scared I was, but did it anyway.

When I presented my keynote in front of a group of 200 people, I reminded myself that I had spoken in front of 30 people before. I reminded myself that this speaking engagement was really just a few more groups of 30. When I did that, the fear calmed down a little. Having a similar experience that I got through without dying, removed the danger factor, letting the brain know that it was OK to move toward this new thing; there was the probability of a safe outcome.

Superpower Activation

#6: CREATING NEW PROOF

Write down 10 ideas/action steps you can take to create new evidence/proof that you can move through the fear.

Next to those 10 ideas/actions, write 1-2 things you've done in the past that are adjacent or similar to the action even if it's from a different area of your life.

You can borrow courage and confidence from other areas of your life and use it in the ones you're still developing. Try it, your brain will feel the relief and it will make it easier for you to take action on the scarier steps.

Throughout the book there are multiple Superpower Activations and Resources - Head to **www.christinecorcoran.com.au/impostor-book** for all the resources mentioned.

Thirteen

DO HARD THINGS

Impostor Syndrome uses your fears against you to keep you safe and ultimately keep you playing small. Have you ever thought, *who do you think you are? You're not (insert not-enoughness story) to do this! You'll be found out. People will see that you're not smart enough/good enough/ knowledgeable enough/pretty enough/experienced enough to do this.*

This internal dialogue feeds into our not-enoughness story and keeps us in our zone of comfort, doing familiar things that lead to familiar results that are "safe". Your brain needs certainty that you're not going to be in danger, it needs to know you've done these familiar things before and survived.

The problem with this is that these safe, familiar behaviours although arguably still important — if done for too long can become the reason you're not moving forward. They're sabotaging your success through familiarity and comfort. Things like admin and website updates are important for your business, of course, but they can become distractions and excuses for avoiding difficult conversations, scary client or collaboration outreach, making connections, or publishing that promotional video.

The worst part is that the story your mind tells you sounds very convincing and true: why put yourself in harm's way by doing hard things, when you could do the safe things and be OK? It's very typical that people fall back into their comfort zone and stay safe. But safety isn't where success lies.

At some point, we must decide that doing the easy, comfortable thing just isn't enough for us anymore. We realise it's not going to get us anywhere we want to be. It's important to be careful because staying comfortable may seem easy now, but done long enough we get stuck. Easy becomes our default, a habit of comfort that only leads to the same results in life.

At some point the comfortable becomes uncomfortable and we realise we're stuck in a habit of sabotage and playing small and the thought of still being in the same place six months later becomes painful.

Ever felt that uneasy, grinding feeling in your chest because nothing is changing?

How long are you going to sit with that unbearable feeling before you decide to push through the fear and familiarity to do the hard things that you know will yield different results?

For some it's days or weeks, for others it's a lifetime of comfort and routine. If you want an extraordinary life, at some point you have to prove to yourself that you can do hard things. Building this resilience comes from choosing courage over fear and taking on the challenge even though it's uncomfortable and uncertain. The important thing is moving through the fear and doing it anyway, as suggested by the title of Susan Jeffers' book, *Feel The Fear...and Do It Anyway*.

So, what hard things have you been putting off lately?

Where have you gotten so comfortable you're frustrated at yourself? Isn't it time to draw a line in the sand and start choosing to do hard things again? That's what made me decide to attend the events in the USA.

It's time to decide that you're going to prove to yourself that you can.

Put it on the calendar, transmute the fear, and take the action.

Superpower Activation

#7: WHERE ARE YOU PLAYING SMALL?

Try this little self enquiry activity to help you determine where you've been playing small.

Make a list of all the hard things you'd like to feel confident about. Of all the things you'd like to do but don't feel capable or qualified to do yet.

Choose one hard thing you've been putting off lately and ask yourself:
- What am I afraid of? Like really? What's the worst thing that could happen?
- Can I make peace with that worse case scenario happening?
- If I don't do this, what will it cost me? What will I not get to experience if I don't do this hard thing? What am I missing out on?
- Will I be proud of myself if I do it?

If the answer to the last one is YES - you have to do it. Now schedule this hard thing in to your calendar this week, or do it today. Don't put it off any longer.

Throughout the book there are multiple Superpower Activations and Resources - Head to **www.christinecorcoran.com.au/impostor-book** for all the resources mentioned.

IF YOU DON'T SHOOT YOUR SHOT, YOU'LL NEVER SCORE.

Now you may be reading this and are unsure if you're playing small. A lot of high achievers experience this response, but trust me, even high achievers hold themselves back, especially when they're surrounded by people doing less than them and praising them for their efforts.

Let's uncover how you could be doing some *harder* things that could quickly level up your results, impact, and expansion.

Think about a big goal you have in mind. One that you think is still a few years off. Ask yourself, *if I was to set out to achieve that goal this year, and I only had five steps to make it happen, what would those five steps be*?

Now 10x that goal and then ask yourself, *if this was my actual goal this year, what action steps would I need to take to make it happen?*

Take some time to think about it and pay attention to the Imposter Syndrome thoughts showing up to cause you to keep you in your comfort zone. Recognise all the inner chatter that happens — all the reasons why you couldn't possibly make your goal happen this year — and if you sit with the goal long enough and focus on it, more answers will come to the surface and big ideas will start to flow.

Could you:
- Pitch to do a Ted Talk
- Pitch to get a meeting with someone who has spoken for Ted before
- Ask for an opportunity
- Put your hand up to speak at an event
- Reach out to invite a new podcast guest
- Pitch to be a guest on a podcast
- Start to share more vulnerably online
- Go live on social media
- Launch that program
- Write that book
- Hire that coach
- Hire that team member
- Reach out to a mentor you look up to
- Elevate your profile through PR
- Show up more consistently
- Voice your opinion on a topic you're passionate about?
- Sell more, promote more

What hard thing would you do?

And that's where you need to tap into your courage and start taking scary action by doing the hard things even when fear is present.

When you become a person that regularly does hard things, the things you thought were hard, become easier and the hard things, become bigger. The more you attribute these courageous actions to who you are as a person, and you become someone this is the norm for, the faster the results start to happen.

You must believe that this is who you are to the core. Someone who does hard things consistently. It's time to believe that you're not only capable of doing hard things, it's part of who you are.

Here is an affirmation to repeat that will upgrade your identity. Repeat it three times throughout the day and see how it impacts your behaviour:

"I am an action taker. I do hard things consistently."

―――――――

Throughout the book there are multiple Superpower Activations and Resources - Head to www.christinecorcoran.com.au/impostor-book for all the resources mentioned.

―――――――

Fourteen

GET LEVERAGE ON YOURSELF

One of the best ways I've pushed through fear again and again is to get leverage on myself. It's hard to give up, give in, or hide when the leverage is so big it would be worse if you didn't take the leap. For some, leverage can be as simple as telling someone important to you what your goal is with the date you want to complete it by. It's hard not to do the thing when people are looking to you to succeed, when your integrity is on the line. For others, having a consequence for not taking an action or a reward to achieving it is a powerful way to motivate action.

If you find it hard to expect more from yourself but you do a lot for others, then declaring your goals and intended actions to someone you value is a good place to start; you'll be more likely to take action on it.

So, how can you get more leverage on yourself?

One way I've done this time and time again is to invest in myself and my business. There have been times when I didn't know how I was going to find the money, but I knew that if I invested in that coach, that mastermind, or event, I was going to level up and my standards would have to level up with me. And time and time again the money has shown up for me because I've levelled up.

I remember a mentor of mine once noticed I wasn't fully committed to taking an action after I had verbally committed and she said, "If I gave you two weeks to get this done, or you'd have to pay me $5000, would you do it?"

"Yes," I replied. I'd find a way.

There's something so empowering that happens when your back is against the wall and you have no other option but to do the hard thing. There will always be more excuses, but getting leverage on yourself removes those excuses and causes you to level up.

Is it time to put your bullshit excuses to the side, and start expecting more from yourself?

What can you do to get leverage on yourself? Motivation to take action on those big scary things doesn't come easy, so this is where leverage can step in to move you into momentum.

Motivation is useless anyway. No one feels motivated to go to the gym, they go because of who they believe they are or what it's going to cost them if they don't. So instead of relying on motivation to get you to do the hard things, start taking action and build on the momentum.

The motivation to keep going will flow.

Here's how to get leverage on yourself:

CONNECT YOUR GOAL TO YOUR DEEPEST WHY

Motivation comes from strong emotional reasons why you want to experience the outcome or result from the action you take. The more connected to your "why" your goals are, the more you're likely to go after them.

To connect your goal to your deepest why, you have to explore it to seven levels of your emotional layers.

This exercise is from the book *Millionaire Success Habits* by Dean Graziosi. The seven layers are used to determine what will really drive you to achieve the level of success you desire.

Ask yourself why it is important to achieve this goal. You'll come up with a reason. With that reason in mind, ask yourself again, *why is that important to me?*

Then with the next answer, ask yourself again, *Why is that important?*

Keep going seven times until you come up with your deepest why. If you get stuck at any point, swap the question out with, *what's the purpose of that? What will that give me?*

Then, with the new answer, go back to the main question, *why is that important to me?*

Once you have uncovered your deepest emotional why, keep it somewhere you'll be able to revisit in times of need or a lack of motivation. The emotional reason why should be powerful enough that you would cut off all other options, excuses, or doubts in taking the action.

A COMPELLING VISION

If your vision is lacklustre, boring, or just not what you actually want, you're not going to want to do hard things to achieve it. Your vision must be a strong and compelling vision that activates you and keeps you on track.

I like to do this 10 years into the future. A ten-year vision can help you realise that you're literally creating your future today and it's up to you to prioritise the action. Anything less than 10 years can feel less compelling and doesn't create leverage to cause you to want to take action now.

When that vision is strong, the leverage you choose to motivate yourself to create action towards your goals just becomes part of the process. Take some time to write out what you want your life to be like in 10 years time and reverse engineer it.

SCORE YOUR COMMITMENT

Once you have your "why" and your vision, revisit your goal and score your commitment. Set a timeframe for this specific goal, and then score yourself out of 10 to discover your commitment level.

Consider 1 as not committed at all, 5 as half committed, and 10 as fully committed, absolutely no doubt in your mind that you're going to make it happen.

Score yourself out of 10 honestly.

If the number is below a five, it might be time to question whether you truthfully want this to be your goal.

If it's between a five and a seven, ask yourself, *what are you afraid of losing if you go all in on your goal? What's the secondary gain if you stay in the same exact same place a year from now?*

As you reflect on this question, you can think of a secondary gain as any motivating factor to not change.

Then ask yourself, *what would have to happen to make it a 10/10?*

This will truly uncover what needs to change, either in your mind or in your life, to be able to fully commit to your goals.

RAISE YOUR STANDARDS

The next step in getting leverage on yourself is to address your current standards and see where it might be time to raise them. Your current circumstances are a direct result of your daily, weekly, and monthly behaviours; standards you expect from yourself. Is it time to do an audit on your standards so you can uncover where your current standards are resulting in your current circumstances?

I remember doing this for myself after hearing Tony Robbins speak about the standards we hold for ourselves at the "Unleash the Power Within" event I attended. We spent a whole hour exploring our standards and I realised that in my mind I thought I was doing everything I could to make the changes I wanted in my life, but my behaviours (standards) were not matching the goals and expectations I had set for myself at all. I had very low expectations of myself and what I was willing to hold as my standards. I was giving up on myself constantly, listening to excuses, and only taking the action when I felt like it.

When it comes to doing hard things, making positive changes, and building new habits in your life, it's very rare that you actually 'feel' like doing something. Exploring the standards I set for my life was such an interesting exercise and it was fascinating to see that in some areas of my life, I was just replicating the same standards my parents had for themselves in the past. In my health, for instance, I had such low standards, and would easily give up on a new health change, diet change, or workout routine. I would find excuses and only work out when I felt motivated, which wasn't very often. I realized, listening to Tony Robbins speak about the standards of elite athletes, high performers, and experts, that they identified their standards and didn't let excuses play into the decisions or when they were going to take action. It became a standard they upheld until it became a habit.

When you explore your standards, identify where your behaviours are not meeting the requirements of the goal and then self reflect to uncover what your standard is there. What do you expect of yourself? Is it a non-negotiable? If not, why? Where do you need to raise your standards and turn the behaviour into a non-negotiable?

Once you raise your standards, you must mentally motivate yourself to build the new habit until it becomes your norm. The best way to do this is to schedule it into your calendar and then work on developing the habit first. When doing this, it's best not to set an extreme goal to begin with, but to focus on developing the habit first.

For example, if your new standard is to prioritise the gym five days a week, let the first week be just getting to the gym five times, don't expect yourself to do a two hour workout with PBs, or go to the extreme because you'll probably hurt yourself or burnout and not get back to the gym the week after. The first week is just focusing on consistency, be gentle in the action. You're more likely to raise the standard on this behaviour if you go gentle in execution and just focus on the habit of visiting the gym five times.

In the process of doing this, I always find it worthwhile to explore the excuses that arise when you're attempting to build the habit. Notice where your thoughts derail you. Notice what challenges arise and work to find the best way to keep the standard strong. If you notice that every Tuesday your work schedule blows out and it's very difficult to get to the gym in the afternoon, you may need to be flexible during these times and change your routine to the morning or another day. Don't set yourself up for failure. Pay attention and be flexible in developing the new standard.

With your thoughts, notice which ones cause you to want to quit, or do something else. Be kind to yourself and ask yourself if it's useful to think those thoughts. You can reframe your thoughts by choosing a more resourceful thought and remind yourself of your why and your vision in relation to achieving that new standard.

Change doesn't come without challenges, know that you're a work in progress and sometimes there are back steps. Focusing on the progress based on yourself yesterday or last month is more supportive than comparing yourself to others, or judging yourself for not being better.

Compassion over judgement leads to positive change.

Superpower Activation

#8: AUDIT YOUR STANDARDS

Audit your current behaviours and standards.
- Identify where your behaviours are not meeting the requirements of the goal and then self reflect to uncover what your standard is there.

Goal # 1: (insert goal here)
- What are your current expectations/ standards of behaviour in relation to this goal?
- What do you expect of yourself?

+ Is it a non-negotiable? If not, why?
+ Where do you need to raise your standards and turn the behaviour into a non-negotiable?

Decide what you want your new standards to be and set out to create a habit of these new standards.

Throughout the book there are multiple Superpower Activations and Resources - Head to www.christinecorcoran.com.au/impostor-book for all the resources mentioned.

ADD REWARDS OR CONSEQUENCES

This then brings me to the fun part. Rewards and consequences.

Some people are motivated by pleasure (rewards) and others are motivated by pain (consequence). Either way, it doesn't matter which one is more motivating for you for this exercise. Sometimes even playing with both can help you to stay on track with your goals and motivate you to keep moving forward. Which would be more motivating for you?

With your goals, or doing that hard thing, determine ahead of time how you're going to reward yourself for taking the action. (Notice I said "taking the action" not "achieving the goal". This is about building the new standards which will eventually lead to meeting your goals and expectations. (Sometimes, though, achieving the goal is out of our control, so focusing on the behaviour is more useful.) Create short-term wins focused on progress and ensure the rewards are supportive of the overall outcome.

Other times, it's worthwhile to create consequences for not taking action. The possibility of a consequence can motivate you to take action to avoid the pain. Whichever feels more motivating for you, add these in as support for getting leverage on yourself.

Superpower Activation

#9: REWARDS AND CONSEQUENCES

Create a list of your goals and next to each one add a reward or a consequence for when you achieve or don't achieve it based on the timeline you set.

Throughout the book there are multiple Superpower Activations and Resources - Head to **www.christinecorcoran.com.au/impostor-book** for all the resources mentioned.

SOCIAL DECLARATION

Another great way to get leverage on yourself is social declaration. If being held to account is motivating for you, then using this tactic can be a game-changer. Keeping your goals and scary big steps to yourself is easy; having no one to keep you accountable just keeps you playing small.

I've used social declaration on so many occasions that I've lost count. Now I have to be careful when sharing something with others to ensure it's actually something I want to do, rather than just an idea I'm still fleshing out. I've shared things I want to do that scare me online, on stages, to people I care about, to people I look up to, and to friends and family, knowing that when that declaration is out there, I have to follow through. I am a woman of my word and will do anything to stay in integrity with this. When someone would follow up with me on something I'd said, and I hadn't made progress on my initial claim, it was the kick up the butt I needed to start taking action on that declaration. Even the potential of being asked about my progress was motivating. If I knew I was seeing the person I had declared something to months ago, I would refocus my attention on that goal to ensure I had something to update them on. Taking it to another level by putting a deadline on the goal and declaration — and then asking someone to keep you accountable — is extremely powerful.

Even while writing this book, I procrastinated. Then one day, I was chatting to a friend who was also writing a book and she shared with me that she was going to be submitting to a specific publisher when their next submission date became available two months later. I responded saying "me too, I'm going to get it done by then," and I kept that date in my mind.

It's supported me in prioritising where to spend my time so I could submit the manuscript at the same time she was. This motivated me and kept me focused and on track with my writing schedule. In early 2024, I embarked on writing this book, and in the process, I also decided to create a TikTok Series on how to turn the Impostor Syndrome into your superpower so I could get leverage on myself to prioritise writing the book.

I know how much life can get in the way, and I had no one keeping me accountable but myself. I declared on TikTok that I would document the writing journey, saying to the world that I was writing this book.

I shared how I would be embarking on a year of growth, and would jump on sporadically and share how I was actively seeking out opportunities to experience Impostor Syndrome knowing this was how I was going to grow. I set the intention to open myself up to more Impostor Syndrome inducing experiences. In the end, this experiment was not just about the social declaration of pursuing Imposter Syndrome for my book, but the powerful intention behind it that has been eye-opening to say the least.

Even though I haven't kept up the documenting on TikTok (only getting to about 17 videos in the series) I kept my word and finished the manuscript within the year. Every time I opened the app it was a reminder to keep writing.

From using the leverage to take scary action, opportunity after opportunity has presented itself in a flow that has not only blown my mind, but confirmed to me that everything I'm teaching you here in this book to turn the Impostor Syndrome into your superpower is a powerful growth tool that can and will change your life. Relying on the tools

I'm teaching you can not only support you to level up, but cause you to upgrade your identity, challenge your thoughts, and overcome fear time and time again.

> THERE IS POWER IN ASKING FOR WHAT YOU WANT OUT LOUD AND SOCIALLY DECLARING IT.

Choose now how you're going to get leverage on yourself to do the hard things that are important to you and start moving the needle in your pursuit of success.

This kind of unapologetic ambitious action will separate you from the 'gonna' people to the successful people. You know those people that say they're 'gonna' do this and 'gonna' do that, but never follow through? I'm sure you don't want to be one of those people so using these tools to expand you and motivate you to take ambitious action, you'll never be one of those 'gonna' people.

Remember that your brain is not wired for growth. It's not wired to want you to do hard things, so getting leverage on yourself will support that courageous action until it becomes part of who you are.

Until then, use leverage and courage.

SURROUND YOURSELF WITH THE RIGHT PEOPLE

And last but not least, surround yourself with the right people. Joining masterminds filled with other action takers and big thinkers has always inspired similar action in me. You've probably heard the famous saying, "you're the average of the five people you spend the most time with," a quote attributed most often to motivational speaker Jim Rohn.

There's also the "show me your friends and I'll show you your future," derivative or even the, "your income is determined by the company you keep." All speak to the same concept: the people you surround yourself with have a powerful influence on you not only directly, but subconsciously, affecting how you see yourself, what you expect from yourself, and how you behave.

We are evolutionarily wired to want to belong to those we surround ourselves with. We build circles of friends around us. Subconsciously, we don't want to negatively impact the dynamic and lose our place or get rejected by our circle. Back in tribe days, if you were ostracised from your tribe, it would surely mean death. That fear is still deeply wired into our DNA; we are aware of what our tribe's rules are, and if we stray from those expectations, we fear being rejected.

If the people you surround yourself with want different things than you, if they judge successful people yet you want to be one, if they have low standards on health, career, or relationships, you're unconsciously going to be adjusting your behaviours to be accepted by those people.

This doesn't mean you have to kick everyone out of your life, no, but it may mean you need to start seeking out more like-minded people who would celebrate the new standard you want to uphold. Spend more time with those who value the same things as you do. Don't disregard the influence of those around you, it can mean the difference between leveling up your life, or staying exactly where you are.

Now you may already have some amazing people who have the high standards you aspire to, and yet, your standards are not shifting. That's when you may need to approach this from a different perspective. Start by coming back to your "why" and your vision. And ask yourself how your circle's insight or support could be helpful. Asking for their support in making these changes could be super beneficial. Be sure to share your goals and declarations with them, ask them to hold you to the new standard, especially if that feels super uncomfortable.

Secondly, you could inspire the new standard or habit by bringing others into your "why" and leveraging it by asking yourself, *what kind of a role model am I being to those I love by playing small here/ by not upholding this standard?*

For instance, your children, friends, and family are also being influenced by you. You are a part of their five people who they surround themselves with, so what standard are you setting for them?

How would you like to influence them? What kind of example would you like to be setting?

If you find this super motivating (or confronting), then let this be the leverage you use to remind yourself when you're giving up or finding excuses rather than taking action on what's important to you. Use it to set the standard and start taking ambitious action.

Superpower Activation

#10: EXPAND YOUR CIRCLE

+ Who do you need on your team? Who do you need in your circle?

+ Create a list of high-value, high-network people that you'd like to connect with.

+ Write a list of people you'd like to spend more time with.

+ Who would you like to declare your goals to?

+ Dedicate time in your calendar and reach out to those people to make the connections. I remember hearing someone on a panel at a conference say how they dedicate every Friday morning to have coffee meetings with new people and I loved that idea.

Throughout the book there are multiple Superpower Activations and Resources - Head to www.christinecorcoran.com.au/impostor-book for all the resources mentioned.

Fifteen

CELEBRATING YOUR WINS

One of the biggest things that perpetuates the Impostor Syndrome is not stopping to celebrate your wins. When you get into the rhythm of working towards the next thing and the next thing, never stopping to take stock and acknowledge yourself for what you have achieved, you keep yourself in a perpetual state of not feeling good enough. This cycle, in turn, keeps Impostor Syndrome holding power over you.

I must say that celebrating your wins is less about popping bottles of champagne, or telling other people how good you are, and more about learning to attribute your skills, abilities, talents, and inner qualities like courage, bravery, tenacity, compassion, strength, kindness, etc, to who you are as a person.

If you don't stop to attribute and acknowledge what you've achieved and the actions you took to make those results possible, you don't add to your bank of evidence or upgrade your identity. This constant pursuit of the next thing keeps you stuck in believing you're not good enough. Acknowledging your wins, no matter how small, is a practice that strengthens your self worth, self belief, and self trust. These three things are very important elements that will set you up for success and allow you to feel deserving of everything you achieve, create, and experience. When you don't celebrate your wins, you are often left feeling like you're never doing enough, that you're never getting ahead, and that you yourself are not enough. Ever felt like that? When was the last time you stopped to reflect and celebrate?

In the world of hustle culture, where we're celebrated for working ourselves into the ground and always striving for more, we quickly burn out. Society conditions us to believe that without a constant desire for more, we're not actively pursuing big things and we constantly feel behind. This keeps us in a cycle of hustle and burnout, wondering when it will ever be enough.

There will always be more to go after. Yet if you only believe you're good enough when you have everything you've ever wanted, or have achieved that next level version of success, you'll never truly feel enough. I want you to learn how to celebrate yourself so you can feel worthy of it all, and believe you're enough, exactly as you are now. That way, you're more likely to go after what *you* want, not just what society deems to be successful.

In my opinion, society celebrates the wrong things. We're conditioned to believe that we're enough when we have the big house, the fancy car, the perfect partner and the 2.5 kids, the six figure income, even if that's not what we actually want in life. And this is where we go wrong: we celebrate the external instead of the internal shifts and upgrades.

We attribute success to the size of our bank account, the six pack of abs, or the perfect body. But if that's not your aligned definition of success, and you're achieving things because you think you have to, it can feel like these achievements aren't worthy of celebrating. All your achievements are worth celebrating, so long as they are in alignment with your goals. Especially the small ones. The steps that create your progress are key.

Our obsession with perfectionism is another thing that can stop us from feeling worthy of celebrating. We always look to make something better, and feel like what we do is not good enough, so we don't celebrate our progress and what we've achieved along the way because it's not perfect yet. Sound familiar? If what we do is not perfect or we didn't hit the exact goal, we prevent ourselves from feeling good for fear it will make us soft.

Some of the biggest lessons I've had so far in my journey of celebrating wins are when I have had my biggest and my worst program launches. Launching (promoting and selling a program online) can be emotionally, physically, and mentally draining. Months of planning goes into launches and it takes a lot of energy to execute on that plan. You're sometimes generating anywhere between three to six to twelve months worth of income in a very short window of time. I have had great launches and I've had terrible launches - it goes hand in hand with online business. Many people launch an offer just once, and when they don't see the massive results they expected, they give up, overwhelmed by the mental challenges required to achieve such big success.

I've had launches that have generated $5K in 30 days, and launches that have generated $76K in 7 days, and everywhere in between; all of them were a success. It's all perspective.

When I did one of my first launches and hit $5K I was over the moon. I was so excited to have hit my goal and have welcomed some beautiful ladies into my program. I remember putting on my favourite song at the time and dancing around my living room with every new sign up! It was finally working, and I was so excited! The energy that I brought to that launch was magnetic and I loved every minute of it.

When I hit the $76K launch, I initially deemed it a failure. Disappointed in the outcome because I had set a goal of $100K and I was $24K off it. I had put my heart and soul into that launch and it was hard!! I had to pivot mid-launch and try a whole bunch of new things because what I normally did wasn't working marketing wise. It was exhausting, and I remember getting to the finish line (last day of the launch) and collapsing in a heap, just deflated.

You'd think that hitting $76K in 7 days would be something that should be celebrated as a major win. I thought I would feel exhilarated, like I'd made it. But I didn't. I felt like a failure.

It wasn't until later that week when I had recovered from the exhaustion, and took the time to reflect on my launch numbers, that I realised I was feeling like a failure because I was measuring the success of the launch against the goal I had set for myself, not the progress I had made.

I had doubled my highest launch numbers and filled my program with the most aligned, incredible dream clients. Just because I hadn't hit the initial goal, didn't mean there wasn't much to celebrate.

This launch represented major progress for me; it was my biggest launch to date. I had tested a new messaging focus which had worked and I had increased the price of my program, plus, I'd attracted an incredible group of women to work with. All in all, a success. Were there lessons learned? Sure. I took the time to debrief the launch with my online business manager and we uncovered what didn't go to plan and things we could do differently next time, but not celebrating this as a win would be a shame.

Beyond debriefing the numbers, I took the time to look at my progress and uncovered the inner qualities that I had leaned on to make this result possible. I thought back to the times I felt like giving up but didn't, and it wasn't until I really reflected on the brevity of what it took to achieve the result, that I allowed myself to feel the joy. I felt immense gratitude for all the women who joined, who trusted me and were willing to invest their hard earned money to work on themselves and their businesses. They could have chosen anyone to work with, but they chose me. That felt pretty special.

I felt proud of myself, I was able to see the full journey: the courage, tenacity, strength, and sheer determination it had taken to reach where I was in business. That's when it truly started to mean something for me. This reflection and celebration allowed me to not only be proud of myself, but allowed me to begin the program with my clients from a place of gratitude rather than frustration at myself for not doing more or not achieving my goals and that meant everything to me.

Without the art of acknowledgement, I would've just moved onto the next goal and quickly filled my days with more goals and actions, thinking I didn't deserve to celebrate yet, not until I hit my big goal. This is when I realised that failing to acknowledge my achievements along the way was the difference between me enjoying my business and hating it.

I didn't start my business to only feel good when I hit those big goals. I had to learn how to enjoy the journey and be proud of myself regardless of the peaks and valleys. Only being happy when I hit the big income goals left a lot of time in between to not feel happy. By acknowledging my progress and then acknowledging the inner qualities that moved me through my journey as a business owner, I felt stronger and more resilient. Acknowledging these inner qualities made them feel like they were a deeper part of who I was. I realised I was going to need these in my pursuit of bigger goals moving forward too.

By allowing myself to celebrate, I felt more confident. I realized that if I was able to overcome all of those challenges in the past, then I would be able to move through them faster in the future and feel more equipped to tackle new challenges. By reflecting, I was able to bolster my self belief in everything I had done and all the action I had taken in the face of fear. I truly felt unstoppable.

Celebrating had nothing to do with shouting my achievements from the rooftops, or even needing to tell anyone else in search of validation, it was for me. It was a deep inner reflection, an act of self love; a much needed act of self love.

Entrepreneurship can be one of the most challenging journeys to embark on, and it requires so much grit, determination, and self belief. To endure the hardships along the way, taking time to celebrate and acknowledge your progress can be the difference between giving up on your dreams or succeeding at them. Most entrepreneurs feel under-appreciated, working their butts off in what feels like a thankless experience. To be brutally honest, it's not up to your clients, family, friends, or anyone else in the world to congratulate or appreciate you for your hard work. It's up to you. Unless you have the ability to be proud of yourself and deeply in love with what you're creating in the world, your motivation will be fleeting. You'll always be wanting more or be left not feeling worthy and underappreciated.

When you learn to acknowledge yourself, to love yourself enough to celebrate yourself, to approve of yourself, then any external validation is a nice cherry on the top, but not a requirement.

In my opinion, learning to celebrate and acknowledge yourself should be a requirement of life. When done right, it's a life skill that builds your self esteem, self belief, self trust, and self love.

When our days are filled with frustration, disappointment, and everyday stresses, joy can feel like a foreign experience — almost like an uncomfortable, unfamiliar feeling — leading us to avoid feeling it. If we haven't practiced feeling of joy when we achieve a goal, the feeling will be fleeting at best. Our mind and body will default to familiar emotions like frustration, disappointment, and stress.

THIS IS WHY CELEBRATING REGULARLY AND BEING PROUD OF YOUR PROGRESS IS SO IMPORTANT.

The more you build celebrations into the journey of business, the more excited and motivated you will feel for your day ahead, and the more you'll be able to enjoy the journey to success.

Don't wait to feel good. Let feeling good, feeling proud, and embracing joy, be part of your everyday experience of business and life. Learning to acknowledge yourself is the best way to build your path to success and not burnout along the way. Allowing yourself to feel the joy of celebrating your wins and progress, is how you do that.

Let's learn the framework for truly acknowledging yourself.

Sixteen

LEARNING TO ACKNOWLEDGE YOURSELF

Every week in my masterminds, I ask my clients to celebrate their wins. I encourage this daily because I believe we need to get in the habit of celebrating and acknowledging ourselves regardless of the milestone. On Fridays especially, I ask clients to reflect on the week that was and find something to celebrate.

Notice how I said "find". I don't give them an option to share a win *if* they have one. No, I ask them to *find* one. There is always something to celebrate, we've just gotten into the habit, or belief, that only big things should be celebrated. It's the small wins each day that should be celebrated more.

Let's be honest, that's where true courage and habits are developed.

Yes we celebrate them signing new clients, hitting goals, or achieving something great, but my favourites are stories where they acknowledge their tenacity, their determination, and their self belief. These are the foundations of bigger changes in their confidence, and success requires bucket loads of that.

I want my clients to celebrate getting back up after being knocked down, motivating themselves after procrastinating, overcoming their fear of putting themselves out there, and showing up for themselves and their businesses. This is where the self belief truly starts to strengthen. After years of seeing my clients practice this type of acknowledgment, it never goes unnoticed by me. Yes I love celebrating their big launches, their income growth, and being booked out months in advance, but when they report back to me how much their confidence has grown, how they now believe in their worthiness, and how much their self belief has expanded, to me that's the ultimate!

I like to teach my clients to even celebrate the failures, the problems, and challenges that arise. In celebrating these hardships, they practice acknowledging the small ways they supported themselves during these difficult times. Teach yourself to celebrate a mindset shift or a change in behaviour, because it's always the small things that lead to big things. If you can't celebrate the small ones, you won't feel worthy of celebrating the big ones.

Your new identity is created everyday in the trenches, doing things you never thought possible. We often overlook these small wins and don't deem them important because they're not big and shiny.

I often have clients who find celebrating wins uncomfortable and argue that they have nothing to celebrate. We're so conditioned by society to only celebrate the *big* wins, the "social media worthy" wins, 100K launches, or hitting a million dollars, that they look at their smaller wins as not worthy of celebrating. Yet to get to these bigger milestones, you need to take smaller actions every day, and you need to believe in yourself and your capabilities to be able to do this consistently.

The best way to strengthen your self belief is to acknowledge what you've done, what wins you've had, how you've overcome challenges, and what inner qualities made all that possible. It's especially important to develop your soft skills. You know the ones, the ones where you talk yourself into taking that scary next step; the one where you pick yourself up after having a hard day; where you show yourself compassion and you speak kindly to yourself instead of judging your shortcomings; when you acknowledge your progress. In my opinion, these skills are so much more important than achieving the big goals.

HERE'S HOW TO DO A PROPER CELEBRATION AND ACKNOWLEDGEMENT:

Step 1: Start by acknowledging the thing you achieved. This could be a small step you've taken, something you've overcome, a problem you solved, or a goal you reached.

Step 2: Acknowledge your inner qualities that made that achievement happen by uncovering what it was inside of you that made the result or outcome possible. Was it your determination? Strength? Generosity? (Insert inner quality here)

Step 3: Reflect on a future goal you want to achieve and recognise how these inner qualities will support you in reaching it.

Here's how this may look:

> I want to acknowledge myself for hitting $100K annual revenue in my business, it was my determination, grit, and passion for helping others that allowed me to achieve this. I know my determination, grit, and passion for helping others will help me in the future as I go after my future goal of hitting multi-six figures in my business next year.

Here's another:

> I want to acknowledge myself for making that difficult phone call. I had been putting it off for over a week and yet, when I did it, it wasn't as bad as I imagined. I'm proud of myself for staying calm and communicating my needs in the conversation so that now I'm on the same page with the other person. It was my courage and empathy that made this possible. I know this won't be the last time I have to have a difficult conversation and my empathy and courage will definitely help me to navigate similar challenges in the future.

#11: ART OF ACKNOWLEDGEMENT

Let's do one together. What's something you've achieved or overcome recently that you would like to acknowledge yourself for? (Can't find one? Look harder. Reflect on each day of this week and you'll find one.)

Write it down.

Then ask yourself, *what inner quality made that possible? Was it your confidence, tenacity, courage, bravery, strength?* Ask yourself now and uncover it. It can be more than one, the more the merrier.

Once you have uncovered your inner qualities, think of a future goal you want to achieve and add the details into this statement:

I want to acknowledge myself for _____(achievement), it was my _____(inner quality) that allowed me to achieve this. I know _____(inner quality) will help me in the future as I go after _____(future goal).

LEARNING TO ACKNOWLEDGE YOURSELF

Now say it out loud to yourself three times. Feel the pride and gratitude for yourself and try to make the feeling last for as long as you can.

Feels good doesn't it? Now start building this into your everyday life. At the end of the day, take a moment to acknowledge yourself for something that day. The more you do this the easier it will become. This practice allows you to rewire your brain to see your progress and feel good about yourself along your journey to achieving your bigger goals.

Throughout the book there are multiple Superpower Activations and Resources - Head to www.christinecorcoran.com.au/impostor-book for all the resources mentioned.

STOP SAYING YOU'RE LUCKY.

In 2024, I was invited to speak at a client's event hosted on a yacht sailing across Moreton Bay. During the interview I was asked, "you've been in business successfully for over seven years now, what makes you different from everyone else that doesn't succeed?"

It was a great question, one that stopped me in my tracks. My first thought was, *I am no different. I'm lucky.*

But before I answered, I took a pause to think of my response before articulating:

Firstly, I am privileged. I was born into a big middle class family, went to a private school, and although money was tight, we never went without, I had opportunities and jobs all my life and was well educated. I was privileged to have my family's backing, and also have grown up in a household that felt safe and supportive.

AND I also worked on my mindset. I didn't rely on anyone else to make my business successful. I demanded it of myself. I didn't allow my mind to go to the place of giving up and I never entertained the thought of getting another job. In the words of Tony Robbins, I 'burned the boats'. I cut off all other options in my mind other than succeeding and I still do this to this day. I don't indulge in self pity or stay too focused on the problem, I look for solutions and take action no matter what, so if that's what sets me apart from others then I'll take that, the power of mindset is everything. It's what determines your end results. It changes your trajectory of life.

LEARNING TO ACKNOWLEDGE YOURSELF

As much as my mind wanted me to say, "I'm not sure, I was lucky," I didn't want this to be my answer because it wasn't luck, it was sheer determination. Even so, I could not ignore my privilege because not everyone is born into my life experience.

LET'S TALK ABOUT "LUCKY"

'WHEN I WON THE OSCAR, I THOUGHT IT WAS A FLUKE. I THOUGHT EVERYBODY WOULD FIND OUT, AND THEY'D TAKE IT BACK. THEY'D COME TO MY HOUSE, KNOCKING ON THE DOOR, "EXCUSE ME, WE MEANT TO GIVE THAT TO SOMEONE ELSE. THAT WAS GOING TO MERYL STREEP."'

— *Jodie Foster*, ACADEMY AWARD WINNING ACTRESS.

Often when I see women being asked about their achievements – or when someone is celebrating them – most shy away from appreciating their success, often calling themselves lucky. If this is society's conditioning of women to make themselves small and not make a fuss, it has to stop. We don't see men say they were lucky, we only see them receive the compliment and celebrate themselves. So why do women say they're lucky?

Whenever I see this happen, I do my best to interrupt and truly acknowledge the woman for what they have achieved. It's often not luck. It's hard work. It's grit. It's tenacity. It's confidence and courage and determination to never give up. Luck implies that it was out of our control. When we really explore how something hard-earned was achieved, we find it has nothing to do with luck at all. So, can we all agree to stop saying we were "lucky"?

YOU WEREN'T LUCKY — YOU WERE A POWERHOUSE!

Seventeen

ACT FROM YOUR FUTURE SELF

Now that we've thoroughly learned to embrace the Impostor Syndrome, I want to share one last tool with you that allows you to accept Imposter Syndrome and not let it hold you back from becoming the person you truly want to become.

You have gotten to where you are today based on your abilities, skills, beliefs, and identity. Every time you came up against something challenging, your brain looked to the past to find certainty in your skills, abilities, and beliefs to see if you could overcome it. When the proof was there, you confidently overcame the challenge. But if it wasn't, you didn't. What if looking to the past was the problem that was holding you back from overcoming new challenges?

When you're stepping into the unknown, doing something you've never done before, there isn't going to be any proof in your past to rely on for a feeling of safety or confidence. Yet, if we focus our attention onto our future self who already has everything we desire – and use our imagination to adopt our future self's beliefs, inner qualities, and values — we're more likely to feel less scared and more confident to take our next step.

When we take the time to imagine that version of ourselves, we can step into their shoes and picture how we would handle a new situation. We can even imagine how we would think, feel, believe, and act from a place of already being successful. So when there's a new experience we have coming up in the future that we're worried or anxious about, we can step into the future and imagine how our future selves would handle it. This is such a powerful practice and one that I come back to again and again.

Doing this allows us to adopt the beliefs, values, and inner qualities of a more resourceful version of ourselves. In doing this, we get a birds eye view of the problem, can tap into our future self's inner resources, and then bring those resources back to the present moment to support a positive action in the now. Our brain doesn't know the difference between real or imaginary, so when you mentally rehearse a scenario, your brain will develop new neural pathways of how to navigate that situation in the present moment.

When we only rely on the past to find proof, we're missing out on adopting the future gifts we can have access to. Not only that, we can miss out on the wisdom our future self has that can support us in the now, especially when it comes to making decisions.

DON'T MAKE DECISIONS FROM THE PAST, MAKE THEM FROM YOUR FUTURE.

When thinking about how to handle a new situation, consider stepping into your future self's shoes to tap into future wisdom that will allow you to take massive aligned action, borrow the confidence and resilience from the future and use it in the now to get what you want. It's another form of reverse engineering your goals.

Let's try it.

Take a moment to imagine your future self living the life you want to be living with all the success, love, and accomplishments that you desire. Imagine these things are in your possession already. Picture how you'll be living your life, who you'll be surrounded by, where you'll be living, what you'll be experiencing. How you'll be dressing, acting, what your days will be life.

Really immerse yourself in that future vision and when it's crystal clear ask yourself, *What does my future self value? What do they believe? What do they prioritise? What do they think about themselves? What are they proud of?*

Now think of a problem you're experiencing in the present, and ask yourself, *what would my future self do here?*

What would the next best step be? What must I value to achieve this next level version of success? Who must I be? What must I do?

The inner wisdom that comes through a visualisation like this can be so much more effective and more profound than any advice a mentor or coach could give you. You already have the answers within you, you just need to learn how to tap into them.

This is a powerful process I love taking my clients through and I've often taken business groups through it as well. It allows you to step into the shoes of your future self and experience an event that hasn't happened yet. Through this exercise, you can see, hear, taste, touch, and experience everything about the moment as if it's already happened. This allows your brain to experience the situation or achievement ahead of time, which ultimately reduces the fear of the unknown and the initial Impostor Syndrome thoughts that pops up when you start moving towards the process in real life.

#12: TAPPING INTO YOUR FUTURE WISDOM

I created a recording for you:

Listen to this audio visualisation and uncover your future wisdom.

VISUALISATION LINK: Find the visualisation via this link: www.christinecorcoran.com.au/impostor-book

---

———————

Throughout the book there are multiple Superpower Activations and Resources - Head to www.christinecorcoran.com.au/impostor-book for all the resources mentioned.

———————

STEP THREE

Seek It Out

Eighteen

LAGUNA BEACH

IF YOU'RE NOT EXPERIENCING
IMPOSTOR SYNDROME YOU'RE NOT GROWING.

It was November 14th 2024, and I was waking up in the most comfortable bed I had ever slept in, in the most luxurious hotel in Laguna Beach, California. I had spent the day before in a recording studio interviewing guests for my podcast, and today I was heading to the last mastermind event for the year with my mentors.

I stepped out of bed, popped on my slippers, and opened the curtains to a glorious day. I had a feeling deep in my belly that today was going to be a great day. I got ready, putting on my outfit that I'd shopped specifically for this event: a brown leather set with a midline skirt, sleeveless top, and colourless shoes. I was feeling excited for what the day would bring.

This time felt different. There were no nerves (I'd honestly had more nerves doing the interviews the day before), no feelings of not belonging, and no doubt that this is where I was meant to be. I made my way to the ballroom where the day would begin and calmly walked in to greet some familiar faces.

The day ran smoothly, meeting new people and reconnecting with those I'd already met; there was definitely a different feeling this time. It may not have looked like it from the outside, but I had changed. It was palpable to me. Remembering back to the first event I attended in Arizona, nine months earlier, not feeling like I belonged, not believing in my worthiness, and feeling way out of my depth. This time I felt at home.

I had set out on an adventure of a year, with intentions of growth and calibration to my next level, and throughout the day my growth was reflected back to me again and again. The expansive conversations, the opportunities presented to me, being invited to speak on future stages, to guest present for big communities, podcast interview requests, and so much more.

I was now the person I had committed to become early that year; the person I had envisioned in my visualisations and meditations; the woman who travelled to the other side of the world to be in rooms like this; the woman who invested in herself, who hired recording studios for her podcast. Suddenly I was the woman who was friends with incredible next level people, someone who could add value to rooms with extremely successful people. I had grown to become someone who accepted opportunities to speak on international stages.

I was finally the woman who counted on herself time and time again.

So much had changed over the year. So much that it would need to be a whole other book to share. But what I will say, is that the intention to grow, the intention to seek out the experiences that would induce the Impostor Syndrome had fundamentally changed who I was and am as a person.

The Impostor Syndrome caused me to level up in so many ways. From how I viewed and went after opportunities, to how I no longer shied away from doing hard things;

I always put my hat in the ring even if I doubted myself. The way I chose to stay and face the fear again and again began to pay off. I raised my rates. I valued myself and my health, losing over 15 kilos throughout the year because my future self valued her health to look her best. The way I dress, the way I invest, the way I show up online, and at events has changed astronomically. I count myself in every time now. When meeting incredibly successful people, instead of putting them on a pedestal, I see myself as their equal. I ask for the opportunities, I don't wait for them to come to me. I create the opportunities, instead of waiting for them to be available. Impostor Syndrome showed up in every one of these scenarios, but I just didn't allow it to derail me. I sought it out and excitedly walked towards it, knowing it was what was going to grow me the most.

Nineteen

CHOOSING CROWTH

Choosing growth is hard. I get it. It would be much easier to just coast along, never challenge yourself, letting the Impostor Syndrome keep you safe in your comfort zone. But how long before it becomes too painful to bear? Human beings require growth, its what keeps us evolving and what makes us enjoy our lives. For example, research on Personal Growth Initiative (PGI)—which involves active and intentional engagement in personal development—has shown that higher levels of PGI are associated with increased well-being and life satisfaction according to **SpringerLink**.

Additionally, Psychologist Carol Dweck's work on the growth mindset indicates that individuals who believe their abilities can be developed through effort and learning tend to be happier and more successful than those with a fixed mindset, as explored by **Nova Psychology**. These findings suggest that pursuing growth and embracing a growth mindset can enhance happiness and overall well-being.

I know you didn't pick up this book just to stay where you are, so I'm sure you value growth too, just like me. The truth is, if you want to grow beyond your current circumstances, or grow faster towards what you want your life to look like, it's much more empowering to let Impostor Syndrome show you where you still have room to grow rather than let it hold you back.

Impostor Syndrome can become your superpower for growth and expansion if you choose to use it that way.

How do you do that, you ask? You learn to use it as a tool for your growth. After everything you've explored in these pages so far, you have learned that the Impostor Syndrome you experience only shows up when you're stepping outside your comfort zone. You now know it shows up to protect you and to keep you safe, but ultimately this protection keeps you living at half your potential.

What if you could see the Impostor Syndrome as a signpost that's saying, "HELLO HI, Yes this is something that is scary but you should totally do it because it will expand you for the better! Imagine who you'll become in the process of doing this?!! Go on, do it."

Putting everything you've learned in these pages into action will allow you to do just that.

You've learned that in taking scary actions, you grow beyond your current limitations and prove to yourself that you're capable of so much more.

When you learn to seek out Impostor Syndrome, instead of avoiding it, you'll expose where you're limiting your potential and where your next big opportunity for growth is.

Now that you know how to navigate the symptoms of Impostor Syndrome, you have all the tools to embrace it when it shows up. It's time you flipped the fear on it's head and used it to call you forward towards expansion. Let's use it as a tool for your growth and success.

IMPOSTOR SYNDROME IS YOUR DOORWAY TO THE HIGHEST FORM OF GROWTH.

Impostor Syndrome only arises when you're pushing the boundaries of who you used to be into who you want to become. When you step outside your comfort zone and attempt to do things you've never done before, the fear kicks in and Impostor Syndrome pulls you back into your comfort zone to stay safe.

But you're not here to play it safe. You're not here to play small. You're here for a big life, to see what you're capable of. You're here to see what could be possible if you took that scary action. You're here to live your life to the fullest. Am I right?

As you continue to strive for success, you'll now expect the fear to show up when you're stretching yourself. You'll know it's inevitable, and if you learn to not only expect it but to seek it out as an expander, that is when it will become your superpower.

You'll be someone who becomes uncomfortable when things get too comfortable because you'll identify that you've stopped growing. Just like adrenaline junkies start to seek out new ways to feel adrenaline, you'll learn to seek out that uncomfortable feeling of growth and expansion by seeking out experiences that induce Impostor Syndrome.

Can you feel it?? The anticipation of that next moment of adrenaline, fear, and excitement all wrapped up into one? That deep inner knowing that something great is about to happen? The suspense of not knowing what's on the other side.

It's intoxicating isn't it?

Now that I've taught you how to expect the Impostor Syndrome and embrace it, it's time to seek it out so it can expand you into living your biggest life.

> IT'S TIME TO BREAK AWAY
> FROM THE MUNDANE.

When you're doing things you've always done do you experience Impostor Syndrome? No, you don't. Your brain already knows how to do those things, and because you've done them so many times before, your brain has the proof from the past of what to expect. Your brain more or less knows the outcome is predictable and safe so there's no fear.

Since there's no danger in the repeated patterns, your amygdala isn't triggered and the Imposter Syndrome remains quiet. But there's no growth in that. Nothing changes when nothing changes. So what if you went after those moments that were, by definition, dangerous in the eyes of Imposter Syndrome?

What if you actively sought out experiences that activated the Impostor Syndrome? What if you used Imposter Syndrome to show you where you can expand and grow?

Superpower Activation

#13: INDUCING THE IMPOSTOR SYNDROME

Let's try it. Get out your pen and paper and answer these questions.

+ What's something you've been putting off for a while that you know will activate Imposter Syndrome?

+ What's something you have contemplated pursuing but doubted if it was possible?

+ What's something you've always wanted to do but you doubted whether you were good enough?

- What's something you dismissed, because you thought you weren't ready?

- What experiences would induce Impostor Syndrome for you?

- Make a list of activities, behaviours, and actions that would inevitably activate Imposter Syndrome for you.

- Write them down now.

- What opportunities would you put yourself forward for?

- What would you ask for?

- What rooms would you choose to walk into?

- What project would you complete?

- What actions would you take?

- What would you create?

- Who would you reach out to?

- What would you do differently each day if you were going after experiences that induced Impostor Syndrome?

- Instead of shying away from these actions, you must move toward them head first.

This is exactly how you turn Imposter Syndrome into your superpower.

Reviewing the list once more, what could be possible for you if you took all of these steps? Did all of those things? What would change in your life? What would change for your business? What would change in how you speak to yourself? In how you view yourself? What would change in what you expect from yourself?

Your life would be expanded on so many levels. You would step up to the plate and raise your hand for opportunities you once shied away from. You'd be creating next level results that blow your mind because you no longer let fear hold you back, you'd believe in yourself more because you'd be taking action on things that scare other people. You'd become a next level version of yourself for sure, and people would start to notice.

Pretty incredible right? This is why you *want* to turn Impostor Syndrome into your superpower. It's your ultimate coach and expander.

Review your list. What do you notice? What thoughts spring to mind?

When you think about taking these actions, does Impostor Syndrome show up already, saying that it's too big for you? Saying you're not good enough? Ready yet?

Remember that you have the tools to support you in navigating the symptoms. You don't have to believe the arsenal of doubt-filled thoughts the Impostor Syndrome will use against you. Trust that you now know how to manage your mind, transmute the fear, and take the action, even in the face of the unknown.

You know that you'll hear the stories that Impostor Syndrome activates in your mind to keep you in your comfort/safe zone, but if you remember to use the tools I've presented to you in this book, you'll become a master at navigating Imposter Syndrome and turning it into your superpower.

This is what successful people do. They don't stop when Impostor Syndrome shows up, they don't let the fear override their decisions and the actions they take, they don't react in fear and stop, they expect it, embrace it, and then they move.

Are you willing to master this skill and move mountains?

With the list you've created above, go back over it and number them. Number them from one, to however many there are on the list.

It's up to you where you start, if you want to put the number one on the easiest and work up to the hardest, or start with the hardest, that's up to you and how courageous you are.

Once you have your list numbered, pull out your calendar, and add these actions to your schedule starting with number one. If you need to break each one down into smaller stages or steps, you can. Either way, there needs to be something on your calendar weekly. Yes, weekly. You're here to play at your fullest, so observe what your mind is saying to you. If you're ready for fast growth, weekly is perfect, but monthly is fine also if you're wanting to stretch out your timeline.

As soon as you start to do this, I'm sure all the excuses from Impostor Syndrome arsenal are going to show up, "I don't have the time", "that week is no good", "I don't have these other things ready (read: perfect) yet", "I'm not ready", "I couldn't possibly" but this is not an exercise of perfection, this is an exercise in courageous action and building the habit of doing hard things. If you need a reminder, read the chapter on doing hard things again.

As soon as you place that action step on your calendar, it's up to you to choose to be resourceful over un-resourceful, remember your training.

Am I going to find a way? Or am I going to find an excuse?

This is your life. You get to choose how you move. Just make sure the moves you make are the ones you're going to be proud of.

Now it's time to choose those big scary actions and make them happen.

Imagine what your life would look like if you continued to seek out the actions that would induce Impostor Syndrome, put them on your schedule, and took action on them on a regular basis?

What if at the beginning of each month, you sat down and asked yourself, *what am I going to do this month that will activate Impostor Syndrome?* Now imagine the results you'll achieve by taking this kind of next level action!

THIS IS HOW IMPOSTER SYNDROME BECOMES YOUR SUPERPOWER. IT'S YOUR EXPANDER.

When you choose to seek it out, it will be the thing that expands you again and again, because, as you've read earlier, Impostor Syndrome doesn't go away no matter how successful you are. Take Meryl Streep for one, you would think after all the years she's been acting and all the movies she's made, you would think she would get to a point where she no longer experiences Impostor Syndrome, but that just isn't the case.

She spoke about this in an interview with Sandy Woznicki of Marie Claire UK, "You think, 'Why would anyone want to see me again in a movie? And I don't know how to act anyway, so why am I doing this?'"

You see, it doesn't go away, but that isn't actually a bad thing. I'm sure Meryl Streep now seeks out projects that will challenge her, that will give her new experiences, and that will expand her. She's ultimately choosing growth, and you can too.

You will continue to experience Impostor Syndrome, but if you use the tools shared with you here, you'll be able to overcome it again and again and continue to level up. It's like a muscle you'll get really good at strengthening, and before you know it, your identity will upgrade too, and you'll become a whole new, next-level version of yourself. You'll level up your goals, make your actions even grander, and expand your life even further.

It all starts with choosing growth over fear. So which one are you going to choose?

Twenty

EVEN HIGH ACHIEVERS PLAY SMALL

Sometimes we don't realise we've chosen to play small. Sometimes the alluring voice of our inner critic lulls us into a fake sense of progress where we do the steps, we get the compliments or accolades, and have all the reasons to believe we're not playing small. It's not until we stop and check in with ourselves to see that in contrast to our fullest potential, we are in fact, operating at 50%.

How do you know when you're playing small?

I find this to be a continuous check-in, a radical honesty practice with yourself. Only you will know if you're limiting yourself. The stronger the relationship you have with yourself, the easier it will become to notice when you're holding yourself back. It all comes back to awareness.

I was at a conference recently, in a room with 250 other business owners and leaders, and I found myself sitting all the way down the back of the room. It was no fault of my own, the seating plan was set, but I found myself sitting low in my chair, getting distracted with my phone, and just not interacting with others at the table the way I normally would.

Was I feeling self conscious? Was I feeling out of my depth? I took a moment to check in with myself. No, I was fine. I felt confident in who I was and how I wanted to show up, I was just tired and it was easier to just relax back in my seat and not engage. But that was not why I was there. I was there to be seen, to engage, to meet new people, and make the most out of the event. There was a reason I had spent $350 to buy the ticket and get in that room. I took myself to the bathroom and splashed some water on the back of my neck, looked myself in the eyes, and reminded myself why I was there. I was allowing myself to shrink and stay comfortable. I observed the inner chatter that was going on in my head telling me that It was OK to be tired, that it was ok to just relax at this event, there would be other events, I didn't have to be so extroverted at every event.

Maybe I was feeling a little of the Impostor? I was finding it hard to connect with the women at my table and I was using that as an excuse to just stay comfortable. I reframed that thought and told myself that just because I didn't connect with the few people at my table didn't mean I wouldn't connect with the other 240 people in the room. I left the bathroom with a new intention to connect with as many of the speakers as possible. After all, they were potential podcast guests. I set my goal as a minimum of 20 connections.

After a little pep talk with this new intention, I strode back into the ballroom, looked around the room, and made a b-line for the speakers. I was no longer going to focus on feeling tired, and gave myself the pep talk I needed to achieve what I was attending the event for: to expand my network with new people. No more dimming my light and blending in.

I find the easiest way to determine if you're playing small is to check in with yourself regularly. Ask yourself, *if I wasn't playing small here, what would I do?*

Your inner knowing will be honest with you if you're radically honest with yourself.

Another way to determine if you're holding yourself back is to review your goals regularly, and create expansion goals to see if you're just taking mediocre action instead of massively aligned, scary action.

Twenty-One
EXPANSION GOALS

During a business workshop event that I was running for women with online and service based businesses in Brisbane, I wanted to put my theory of playing small to the test. One of the ladies in the room volunteered to let me use her business as an example.

Everyone in the room was focused on the flipchart where I mapped out her goals for everyone to see. They were modest goals. She was wanting to convert 100 new members into her membership, hit $150,000 in revenue, and increase her following on social media.

To do this she had mapped out some action steps to help her achieve these goals. It looked something like this:

- *Post on social media regularly*

- *Attend networking events*

- *Run a quarterly workshop to attract new members*

- *Do some Instagram lives and*

- *Be active in Facebook groups where her ideal client was hanging out.*

Despite her ambitious goals, and seemingly clear action steps to achieve them, this business owner was only converting 15-20 members annually.

The business owner's logic was this: *if I do it more consistently, and have a better strategy, then maybe it will work.* She wasn't happy with her current results which were, of course, the result of her current action steps. For her to create different results, she was going to have to do something different. To create better results, she was going to have to start thinking bigger. To help her do that we mapped out an expansion goal so she could see where she was falling short.

To preface this activity, I asked her to play along and not get caught up in the mindset chatter that would inevitably show up as we created her expansion goal.

I flipped the chart over to a new fresh page and wrote at the top of the crisp white paper:

Expansion Goal = 1000 New Members

Her eyes widened a little as I smiled back at her and said, "Now imagine that your new goal for this year ahead is not to convert 100 new members, but to convert 1000 new members. Take a moment to really think about it. If this was your actual goal, what action steps would you take?"

She paused for a moment. I could see her mind ticking over. She brought her hand to her mouth and she pondered this new goal before she said,

"If 1000 members was my goal, then I'd probably get more strategic with my content for social media and I would make it a non-negotiable to post consistently. And then I would research bigger events to attend and have a goal for each one to gain people's information to grow my email list. I would create a plan to follow up with them to see if the membership is the right fit for them. I'd probably even start my own Facebook Group and use it to run some challenges to attract new people there as well."

Now she was thinking more strategically. I asked her to keep going as we added bigger action steps to the flip chart. Shortly after she came to a pause and I could see that her mind was going blank. She wasn't able to come up with any more ideas, so I asked, "Instead of running quarterly workshops, why not do monthly?"

"Oh I couldn't," she said.

"Why not?" I asked.

She stood there unsure of what to say. I asked her again, "What else could you do to get in front of potential new members?"

Again she was coming up blank, so I put it to the audience. The floodgates began to open. New idea to new idea started to flow:

EXPANSION GOALS

- I would pitch to be a guest on podcasts where your ideal client listens and offer a juicy lead magnet to grow your email list and your visibility

- I would pitch some article ideas to some online publications and get your business out there on a bigger scale

- I would pitch to speak at events where your ideal client is attending so you can become known to your ideal client

- I would pitch to other business owners who have similar or different communities to be a guest presenter. Other groups could benefit from the workshops you run. That's a great way to get in front of new audiences

- I would find other businesses that have a strong online following and pitch to do a joint Instagram or Facebook Live so you can get in front of new audiences

- Host your own podcast and invite high level business owners (who have a similar audience) to come and be a guest on your podcast

+ I would create a new lead magnet every month and add lots of value to your ideal clients as I'm sure they'll share it with their friends who have a similar goal

+ I would start Facebook ADs to the membership sales page or to your lead magnet and put them in a sales funnel

+ I would start an affiliate program and invite other successful business owners (who don't offer what you offer) to join so they can sell for you.

And the ideas just kept coming.

My brave attendee stood at the front of the room with her jaw almost on the floor. She hadn't thought of any of these. At that moment she realised she was playing small. She was just taking mediocre action for mediocre results. It was time she stepped up to the plate to take bigger actions.

Most people underestimate what it takes to achieve their goals and just do what everyone around them is doing. Setting an expansion goal is a great way to not only think bigger, but to really uncover some great ways to grow your business.

I regularly take my mastermind clients through this activity for that exact reason; to uncover some next level action steps that could catapult their results.

AVERAGE GOALS = AVERAGE RESULTS

"Most people overestimate what they can accomplish in a year – and underestimate what they can achieve in a decade!"- Tony Robbins

Write down your goals as specifically as you can. Whether it's a financial goal, milestone goal, or impact goal (amount of people you want to impact). Be as specific as you can. If you cannot measure if you're getting closer or further away from your goal, it's not specific enough.

Write down a timeline for your goals. Next to your goals, write down the date you'll achieve them by.

Once you have them clearly written down, I want you to create an expansion goal by multiplying that goal by 10 just like I did with my attendee, we went from 100 new members to 1000 new members.

Then ask yourself, *If this was my actual goal that I was going to work towards, what action steps would I take to make this happen?*

Write down all the ideas that come to mind. Aim for a 10-minute session to unlock a flood of amazing ideas. You could also put the goal and the question into AI and see what ideas come up that you haven't thought of. Ask a friend what they think.

It is completely OK for you to *not* actually want to achieve that 10x'd goal, but that's not the point of this exercise. The point of the exercise is to determine if you're playing it safe with the actions you're currently taking.

This exercise will highlight if you're taking mediocre action/small steps or if you're truly being ambitious and determined in achieving your next level goals.

Then ask yourself, *if this was my actual goal, how would I feel?*

Notice what your brain throws at you. Write it down. In fact, write down all the fear thoughts that show up and all the reasons why you think this goal is not achievable for you.

After I got all the ideas from the audience, I turned to my attendee and could see that she was looking at the list with fear in her eyes.

I reminded her that she didn't have to act on all of these ideas. This was just an exercise to highlight what she could be focusing on in order to get bigger results. A lot of the things on the list she didn't feel ready for and I could see the Impostor Syndrome thoughts were running rampant in her mind. So I asked her what her thoughts were based on, fear or resources?

She looked at the list again and then explained that some were resources, she didn't have the money or the know-how for Facebook Ads. Others were fear based, she didn't feel expert enough to pitch to online publications to write an article.

Reflect on all the reasons you wrote down. Are your thoughts based on resources or fear?

If all the reasons you wrote down are based on fear, such as not feeling ready, good enough, or doubting if it's possible to achieve the goal within the timeframe, then you've got some fear to overcome and some room for growth. If your reasons are based on resources, like not enough time, money, energy, clients, team, etc, then ask yourself: How can I be more resourceful here?

You're either getting in your own way or not being resourceful enough with the resources you do have access to.

After taking my attendee through this exercise it was so clear what fears were holding her back, where she had to grow, and all the opportunities she had at her disposal to achieve her goals.

Similar to this Tony Robbins quote above, not only do we overestimate what we can achieve in a year, when we're not stepping into our full potential, we underestimate what we can achieve when we give ourselves less time. Most people overestimate how much time things will take and give themselves longer to achieve it, possibly safeguarding themselves from failure or putting the failure off. To determine if you're doing this, using the same goals, reduce the time and see what fears show up.

If you gave yourself six months to achieve that goal you wrote down, ask yourself, *if I was to achieve this goal in half the time, what would I do differently?*

Another way to do this is to reduce the steps. If you only had five action steps to make that goal happen, what steps would you take?

This is such a great exercise to truly uncover where you're staying in your comfort zone and to be honest, most of us are holding ourselves back and playing it safe. Most of us let fear get the better of us and continue to live a life taking average action and living an average life. So please, I implore you, don't let your life be one of comfort and safety. Let it be expansive. By doing these self reflections and check-ins regularly, you'll start to expect more from yourself.

Lastly, the final little check I do with this exercise is to again review what you've written down and notice where you took yourself out of the race before it even began.

What goal did you think of but didn't write down, knowing that you were going to have to reflect on yourself and your progress?

What idea did you have that you didn't even write down, thinking you weren't good enough to do it?

What action step did you think but again didn't write down because you didn't think you could do it, or thought it was too big, too risky?

Why did you not write these down?

Don't count yourself out before you've even tried.

This exercise can be uncomfortable. It can show us where we're operating at half our potential and can ultimately bring up feelings of self doubt, self judgement, and self disappointment. These are often feelings we want to avoid.

FEAR IS OFTEN PROTECTING US FROM FEELING THESE UNCOMFORTABLE FEELINGS.

We all want to feel the joy and excitement of an accomplishment, of winning after doing the big scary things, but none of us want to feel the pain of disappointment, shame, rejection, and judgement. It's the thought of potentially having to feel those feelings that keeps us stuck, doing what we've always done. But what if life was about experiencing the full spectrum of human emotion?

By avoiding feeling those negative emotions of disappointment, what if it meant you'd also miss out on feeling those feelings of euphoria, exhilaration, and fulfilment, too?

The only reason we fear feeling negative feelings is because we're not taught to process them in a healthy way.

According to the Adverse Childhood Experiences (ACE) Study (Felitti et al., 1998), many individuals were brought up in households where parents didn't know how to model a healthy way of processing emotions and emotional regulation, so children only learned to repress or suppress emotions, leading them to build up and build up, until the emotions became too big to feel.

When children grow up in environments where healthy emotional regulation is not modelled (e.g., when parents suppress or ignore emotions), they are more likely to internalise maladaptive strategies like emotional repression. Over time, this leads to emotional buildup and difficulty managing overwhelming feelings.

When we learn to process our emotions in a healthy way — at the time we feel them — the emotion can move through our body within about 90 seconds. It's when we don't process our emotions, we hold on to them, not really knowing how to feel them, that our emotions can stay stuck and we eventually put off experiences that could bring up past pain and unprocessed emotions.

Instead of suppressing or repressing our emotions, we must learn to feel them, be present with them, accept them by acknowledging how we feel, and be kind to ourselves in the process of feeling them. We must stop judging our emotions as negative; they're not good or bad, they're just feelings that need to be expressed so they can move through our body to be processed.

When we do this with unconditional love for ourselves, there is no emotion too big to feel. And yes, having support to process the big emotions that you've suppressed or repressed for years is ideal. Often we don't know what to do with our feelings or how to move through them, so seeing a therapist to support you in this is the highest form of self love.

Once you've processed the old past emotions, you can learn to accept the emotions that happen in the present, and be able to process them in real time. Doing this will allow you to see how you're able to feel any emotion that arises, and when you can do this, you won't fear them.

Don't take yourself out of the race before you've even begun because you're afraid to feel a potential emotion in the future.

Eventually you realise that the worst thing that can happen is not that big scary failure or dangerous outcome. It's just a feeling. And you can handle a feeling.

"THE WORST THAT CAN HAPPEN IS A FEELING. NO MATTER WHAT HAPPENS, I'M GOING TO BE OKAY, BECAUSE THE WORST THAT CAN HAPPEN IS AN EMOTION, AND I KNOW HOW TO EXPERIENCE EMOTION."

— *Brooke Castillo*, MASTER COACH INSTRUCTOR AND FOUNDER OF THE LIFE COACH SCHOOL & PODCAST

Superpower Activation

#14: CREATE AN EXPANSION GOAL

EXPANSION GOALS

Take some time to flesh out your expansion goals and bring awareness to where you're playing small so you can start taking big ambitious action towards your goals.

To create an expansion goal, write down your realistic goals and times them by 10.

Then imagine that this new goal is your actual goal and write down everything you would do to create that result. What would you prioritise and what would your steps be?

Then, reduce the timeline. If your goal was a 12-month goal, reduce it to six months and write down everything you would do to make it happen in that timeframe.

Lastly, take the rocking chair test.

Take a moment to picture your long-term future, when you're 85 or 90, sitting on your porch in your rocking chair reflecting on your life, are you going to regret not taking that action? Are you going to regret trying?

Are you going to be happy with how you let fear win?

Don't count yourself out of the race before even trying, you've got a whole life to live and giving something a go is something you can be proud of yourself for so when you look back. You will know that you squeezed every inch of life out your years.

The last thing you want to feel at the end of your life is regret. Yes, the potential failure might be bad, but not trying is worse.

In my opinion, regret is worse.

You'll never regret taking action and showing yourself what you're capable of.

———

Throughout the book there are multiple Superpower Activations and Resources - Head to **www.christinecorcoran.com.au/impostor-book** for all the resources mentioned.

———

Twenty-Two

THE IMPOSTOR SYNDROME IS YOUR SUPERPOWER

"YOU WALK INTO A ROOM AND HAVE THE THOUGHT, 'I DON'T BELONG HERE'. WE REQUIRE THAT FEELING."

—*Lori Harder*, FOUNDER, OF GLOCI AND HOST OF THE *EARN YOUR HAPPY PODCAST*

You have the power to change your life every single day and that power lies in your mind. Through these pages you've learned that Impostor Syndrome is not an affliction or incurable disease, it's a psychological phenomenon that happens in the mind. It's a fear based thought patten that keeps you stuck in your comfort zone unless you choose to change the narrative, but you now know to expect it and you won't be surprised when it shows up.

You've learned that you have the ability to embrace the fear response you'll inevitably encounter when you choose to step outside your comfort zone in the pursuit of growth by transmuting that fear into something more useful. You know that growth and fear are a packaged deal and to live an extraordinary life you'll have to learn to be OK with being uncomfortable because that's where the growth happens.

You've learned how to flip the script on the arsenal of thoughts the Impostor Sydnrome throws at you and how to rewire your brain for courage and expansion. You're discovered that you're more than capable of doing hard things and building a bank of evidence to remind you of your greatness and capability will keep your mind strong and strengthen your self belief every step of the way. You now know that celebrating your wins is not a self indulgent act, but a necessity to keep the Impostor Syndrome at arms length so you can update your identity with every new milestone you experience to keep you moving forward.

You've learned to truly acknowledge yourself and your progress and how to tap into your future self so you can become the person who has the life you want to be living. You'll speed up the process of becoming because you now have the tools to expect, embrace and seek out the Impostor Syndrome to live a life of your dreams. It's time to expand and start challenge the norm, by expanding your capacity for more and putting yourself in experiences and rooms that are designed to stretch you.

Because let's be honest, If you're putting yourself in rooms (circles, groups, organisations, places) that don't make you feel like you're the smallest fish in the pond, you're probably operating at half your potential. If you're the smartest, the best, the most successful in the room, what will you learn from that room? Most likely nothing. You'll end up subconsciously trying to belong by being more like the smaller fish. In doing this, you'll end up with smaller results, just like them. But you don't stand for that anymore. Just like my standards, expectations and beliefs have grown, so have yours, and it's up to you to hold that standard of yourself high.

As we kicked off the event in Laguna Beach, our mentors took to the stage and spoke to the experience of being in a room with like-minded people and how to make the most of an experience when you're surrounded by a plethora of successful people doing great things. They congratulated everyone for choosing to be there and then spoke about how they, as a couple, actively seek out rooms just like this, speaking to the fear of not feeling like they belong, and letting that feeling be the confirmation that they're in the right rooms.

They're actively seeking out experiences that induce Impostor Syndrome, knowing it is what will expand them. In that first room at the beginning of the year, I had multiple moments where I didn't feel "enough", yet I didn't let it stop me from learning and connecting. I could have easily flown home the next day and decided not to return, to be a slave to those uncomfortable feelings, but I chose differently.

I even had a moment in October where I thought about not flying over for the last event, and was called out by one of my friends about my commitment to my next level, (thank you social declaration and to that friend) because it was a beautiful reminder of my commitment to growth and to this book.

I was holding myself back and knew it would be more comfortable to find a great excuse to not go, but instead I found a reason to attend, and waking up the next morning after the event, I had a moment of absolute gratitude because the expansion that happened that day was mind blowing.

I had set out this year to seek out Impostor Syndrome and let it expand me, and I had done just that. I stretched myself, made the big asks, got myself in the rooms, and landed the opportunities with so many more to come, and I could feel the shift where my identity truly had evolved.

I can look back now at who I was when I started this year and I now see a different person. I'm so proud of myself for having the courage to continuously seek out growth over fear. Using the tools I share with you in this book, you can do this too.

It's about learning to be comfortable with the uncomfortable, to not believe everything your mind throws at you, and to take back control of your life.

When we're not willing to do the things that give us uncomfortable feelings, we're only experiencing a life half lived. At the end of the day, life is 50/50. It's not all positive and it's not all negative, and how you view it is up to you. You can judge your emotions as bad, and be a slave to how you feel, or you can embrace every feeling as an opportunity to experience all that life has to offer.

Deep down you want it all, and giving yourself permission to feel it all allows you to embrace life, move through the feelings, and keep participating fully. That's how we live a fulfilled life. Let it all be fulfilling: the good, the bad, and the ugly. Turning the Impostor Syndrome into your superpower is just one way to not let your emotions dictate your life.

It's all a choice. A choice of how to view things, how to react, and how to respond. A choice of intention. When we give in to the fear, we're letting it cloud our options and limit our potential. We begin to think that when fear hits, we should stop because there may be danger. But there could also be joy, love, opportunity, and expansion. There could also be lessons, growth, and new beginnings. How you see it is up to you.

So don't believe everything your mind tells you. Question it, and choose again.

You get to choose. Choose to see your Impostor Syndrome as your superpower for growth and expansion.

THE IMPOSTOR SYNDROME IS YOUR SUPERPOWER

SEEK IT OUT.

CHOOSE TO SEE YOU'RE GOOD ENOUGH JUST AS YOU ARE.

CHOOSE TO SEE YOU ARE WORTHY NO MATTER WHAT.

CHOOSE TO ACT IN THE FACE OF FEAR.

CHOOSE TO FEEL IT ALL.

CHOOSE TO LIVE FULLY.

THANK YOU & YOU DON'T HAVE TO STOP HERE

Thank you so incredibly much for taking the time to read or listen to my words and be a part of this journey. If we've connected in the past or are currently connected, I hope these pages inspired you with courage and excitement for a big life ahead, and fueled your ambitions. If we're not connected just yet I hope you take the first step and reach out, I'd love to connect with you and find out about your big dreams so I can cheer you on and celebrate your growth.

There is so much life to live and I hope you have the courage to live it fully.

If you'd like to delve deeper into this work or would like the accountability to choose courage over fear, and are ready to take your business to the next level feel free to reach out to me on social media, or you can find out all about the programs I run and 1-1 coaching offerings via my website.

www.christinecorcoran.com.au

LET'S WORK TOGETHER

If we're not friends on socials yet, please connect, I'd love to hear your biggest takeaways from this book.

CONNECT HERE:

INSTAGRAM:
WWW.INSTAGRAM.COM/CHRISTINECORCORAN_COACH

FACEBOOK:
WWW.FACEBOOK.COM/CHRISTINECORCORANCOACH

Remember to get all the resources connected to the book here: www.christinecorcoran.com.au/impostor-book

Acknowledgements

If it wasn't for my incredible clients none of this would have been possible so I must start there. I get to work with the most genuine, kind and generous women in business who inspire me every day. They are ambitious yet humble and they make me want to be a better coach and a better human being. Every day I am inspired to bring the best version of myself to our sessions, to upskill constantly and create breakthrough programs that support them to live their lives to the fullest. If you're a current, past or future client of mine, I want to say thank you. Each and every one of you have inspired this book and inspired in countless ways and you encourage me to live a bigger life and I appreciate your support with this book so much. I want to be the example of what's possible when you work on your mindset and go after your dreams so I hope that this book inspired you to dream bigger, reach for your fullest potential and prove to yourself what you're capable of. Because you my friend, are capable of absolutely anything!

To my Mum, and my beloved Dad thank you for giving me everything I have needed to live the life I have created. Thank you for always supporting me, for showing me what's possible when you work hard, and for always believing in me. Thank you for encouraging me to see the world and go after my dreams.

I hope I've made you proud.

To my sisters - thank you for always supporting me. For encouraging me and for telling me that you're proud of what I have created and the life I have forged for myself. Thank you for always being my sounding board, cheerleaders and uplifters.

To my whole family and friends, thank you for supporting my dreams, and always seeing the best in me. Thank you for challenging me to grow and giving me the opportunity to learn and develop myself. Your support means the world to me. Thank you from the depths of my heart. I appreciate you beyond words.

About the Author

Christine Corcoran is a dynamic and passionate Business Strategist and Master Mindset Coach, dedicated to empowering ambitious female entrepreneurs to scale their businesses with ease and authenticity. With over a decade of experience in business development, Christine has helped hundreds of women break free from their limiting beliefs, refine their sales strategies, and create scalable offers that support their dreams of financial abundance and personal freedom.

Christine's transformative coaching programs and sought-after retreats have become a beacon for business owners ready to align their goals with their values, embrace unapologetic ambition, and lead with confidence. Known for her authentic approach, she blends actionable strategies with deep mindset shifts, encouraging her clients to dream big and execute fearlessly.

Beyond building a successful multi-six figure business, Christine was named Coach of the Year finalist in the Beam Business Awards, is a dedicated podcast host of The Next Level Life Podcast, keynote speaker, and visionary behind the Unstoppable Sales Program & Next Level Mastermind. Her inspiring journey—marked by resilience, bold leaps, and a commitment to personal evolution—has positioned her as a trusted leader in the entrepreneurial space. Whether speaking on stages or guiding clients through breakthrough moments, Christine's mission remains steadfast: to help women build thriving businesses and lives they love.

Christine resides on the Gold Coast, where she balances her thriving business with a life of adventure and connection. When she's not coaching or writing, you'll find her hosting transformative events, crafting powerful mindset tools, and hanging out at the beach or connecting with her community of unstoppable women.

To work with Christine or to hire her as a speaker—head to www.christinecorcoran.com.au

www.ingramcontent.com/pod-product-compliance
Lightning Source LLC
Chambersburg PA
CBHW071954070526
44583CB00015B/1190